The Poetry of Arab Women from the Pre-Islamic Age to Andalusia

This is a compilation of poetry written by Arabic women poets from pre-Islamic times to the end of the Abbasid caliphate and Andalusia, and offers translations of over 200 poets together with literary commentary on the poets and their poetry.

This critical anthology presents the poems of more than 200 Arabic women poets active from the 600s through the 1400s CE. It marks the first appearance in English translation for many of these poems. The volume includes biographical information about the poets, as well as an analysis of the development of women's poetry in classical Arabic literature that places the women and the poems within their cultural context. The book fills a noticeable void in modern English-language scholarship on Arabic women, and has important implications for the fields of world and Arabic literature as well as gender and women's studies.

The book will be a fascinating and vital text for students and researchers in the fields of Gender Studies and Middle Eastern studies, as well as scholars and students of translation studies, comparative literature, literary theory, gender studies, Arabic literature, and culture and classics.

Wessam Elmeligi is Assistant Professor NTT at the Department of Classical Mediterranean and Middle East at Macalester College in St. Paul, Minnesota, and Associate Professor at the English Department, the Faculty of Education, Damanhur University, Egypt. With a PhD in literary theory, his research interests include comparative literature, narratology, psychoanalysis, gender and women's studies, visual analysis of film and art, digital humanities, as well as translation. He has published articles and book chapters on Naguib Mahfouz, Radwa Ashour and the modern Arabic novel, Bernard Shaw and Arabic adaptations of the English theatre, and the *Arabian Nights*. He has also written and illustrated two graphic novels, *Y&Y* and *Jamila*.

Focus on Global Gender and Sexuality

Trans Dilemmas
Stephen Kerry

Gender, Sport and the Role of the Alter Ego in Roller Derby
Colleen E. Arendt

The Poetry of Arab Women from the Pre-Islamic Age to Andalusia
Wessam Elmeligi

Interviews with Mexican Women
We don't talk about feminism here
Carlos M. Coria-Sanchez

www.routledge.com/Focus-on-Global-Gender-and-Sexuality/book-series/FGGS

The Poetry of Arab Women from the Pre-Islamic Age to Andalusia

Wessam Elmeligi

Routledge
Taylor & Francis Group
LONDON AND NEW YORK

First published 2019
by Routledge
2 Park Square, Milton Park, Abingdon, Oxon OX14 4RN

and by Routledge
605 Third Avenue, New York, NY 10017

First issued in paperback 2020

Routledge is an imprint of the Taylor & Francis Group, an informa business

British Library Cataloguing-in-Publication Data
A catalogue record for this book is available from the British Library

Library of Congress Cataloging-in-Publication Data
A catalog record for this book has been requested

Typeset in Baskerville
by Apex CoVantage, LLC

ISBN 13: 978-0-367-72806-9 (pbk)
ISBN 13: 978-1-138-32357-5 (hbk)

For those of you who
Scribbled poems on a wall,
Wishes do come true.
Believe the poems, then.
For I believe them all.

Contents

4   Poets of the early Islamic period   51

5   Analysis: poetics of rejection   61

Acknowledgments

I remain indebted to all my professors at the University of Alexandria, especially my mentor Professor Amira Nowaira. Most relevant to this book are Professors Helmy Heliel and Ahmed El-Sheikh, who taught me the value of translation. I am always grateful to Professor Maria DiBattista for her constant support. I benefited tremendously from the insights of Professor Mustafa Mughazy, whose remarkably lucid work on translation practices has been invaluable to this book. I am privileged to have always had intelligent and talented students at Alexandria University, Damanhur University, Pharos University, the Arab Academy, Middlebury College, and Macalester College. My colleagues in those institutions provided me with much needed collegiality and friendship. I appreciate the tireless work of the amazing library staff at Macalester College, especially Aaron Albertson, Connie Carlen, and Ginny Moran, and the indispensable guidance of Alexandra McGregor, Katherine Imbert, Eleanor Catchpole Simmons, Autumn Spalding and the editorial team at Routledge. My family gets all the credit for shaping a person who wants to write a book about Arab women poets.

1 Introduction

Writing a critical anthology of women poets in translation

In this introductory chapter, I comment on the process of writing this book. As a critical anthology of poems in translation, the book concerns itself with issues of presentation, authenticity, analysis, and translation. All four elements combined serve the main purpose behind this project: to offer a glimpse at the poetry of Arab women who were enriching the cultural scene of a period of history that is often studied in contemporary academia with interests that often do not prioritize the literary significance, and at times even the literary contribution, of Arab women to begin with.

Presentation

Anthologizing classical poetry is an arduous task. It might become even more so if the task is paired with translating the poems. What makes the task particularly challenging for this specific project, however, is a third element: gender. Anthologizing classical women's poetry is also an unavoidable research in representation. Searching for, reading, translating, and commenting on these marvelous poems by Arab women is a journey in various aspects of representation. Self-representation is naturally a primary theme here, as the poets project their identities on their verse. Yet, there is another significant aspect of representation involved: the position of women in their communities. The communities that these women lived in are created in their poems, shedding some light on the societal perception of women from the perspective of the women themselves. In order to reflect these sinewy changes, one of the main objectives of this book is to offer some insight to how women wrote their poems within the contexts of their daily lives. Therefore, the poems of each poet are translated as part of a brief narrative and commentary on the poet's life and the circumstances of writing the poems, if they are known. In addition, the selection intentionally covers poems by several lesser known poets, the majority of whom have never been translated in English before, thus casting a wider net that might reveal more details that are harder to decode in the "official" stories of the few mainstream Arab women poets who have been translated so far, and who are also still included in this book, but perhaps contextualized rather more realistically now that they are presented with their lesser-known contemporaries and their narratives.

Authentication

The development of anthologizing Arab women's poetry over the past several hundred years cannot be underestimated. For example, one of the prime anthologists of his time, al-Aṣfahānī, clearly distinguished between free women poets and slave women poets, as is indicated in two separate projects he wrote, *Al-Imāʾ ash-Shawāʿir* (*Female Slave Poets*) and *Akhbār an-Nisāʾ* (*The News of Women*) in his bigger and best-known project *Kitāb al-Aghānī* (*The Book of Songs*). This adds socio-economic class as a major consideration. Modern anthologies tend to divide the poems chronologically, a classification that this book maintains, with designations such as pre-Islamic, Umayyad, and Abbasid. In order to make use of the different skills, objectives, and achievements of classical and modern anthologies, the selection process initially followed a strict authentication method that involved confirming that every poet, and poem, are mentioned in at least one modern and one classical source. There was no need to set that minimum requirement. All poets and poems were found in more than one modern and more than one classical source. The sources used in the selection process of the poets, their biographies, and their poems in each chapter are all listed in the bibliography at the end of that chapter.

Analysis

The thematic variety of classical Arab women's poetry is often neglected in literary studies of Arabic poetry in translation. In reality, tracing such variety can be a rewarding experience of the literary heritage of the classical period and the cultures that thrived during that time. A case in point is that the focus on elegies and battle motivation in poetry written by women in what is referred to as pre-Islamic poetry and crossover poetry can be sharply contrasted to a wider range of poems, from Sufi and spiritual poems, to wine and erotic poetry, starting from the Umayyad period. In order to understand this growth, the book draws an invisible line between the pre-Umayyad and Umayyad period, as well as introduces what can be termed crossover poets, for poets who wrote during the transition from pre-Islamic to early Islamic literary scenes. I attempt a comparative analysis after the chapters on pre-Islamic, crossover, and early Islamic poetry, on the one hand, and Umayyad, Abbasid, and Andalusian poets on the other hand. Such analysis reflects a change in the cultural role played by women over that period of time, from mourners to courtesans, to saintly figures and lovers, and, equally important, notes the level of cultural agency they acquired.

Translation

The original duality of translation that started with St. Jerome's notion of meaning-for-meaning as opposed to word-for-word has defined approaches for translation for centuries (Bassnett and Lefevere 2). While its basic outlines survive, it has developed and has become more complex, with notions of acculturation and various degrees of faithfulness to form and message alternating their central place in the spotlight of debates over translation strategies in the field of translation studies (Lefevere 109).

Among all forms of translation, "the translation of poetry is held to be the most difficult, demanding and rewarding form of translation." Connolly reiterates that it is widely maintained that the translation of poetry is a special case within literary translation and involves far greater difficulties than the translation of prose (171). Within this project of interlingual translation, defined by Jakobson as a translation between distinct languages (in this case Arabic and English), there is, at least to some extent, another process of intralinugal translation, or the translation from one historical period to another of the same language (which in this case is translating classical poetry for 21st-century readers) and the project becomes more complex, but also more interesting (232–39).

The basic philosophy behind translating these poems is choice. A translator has to make choices to minimize loss and to strike a middle course among various extreme strategies. There are key notions that I had to take into consideration when making these choices. An important understanding is the distinction between levels of fidelity to the original text on the levels of poetic form, message, and word choice. Dickins, Hervey, and Higgins refer to degrees of bias towards the source text (ST) or target text (TT). In that context, interlinear translation displays extreme bias to the source text where TT does not necessarily respect ST grammar (15). Literal translation is a diluted form of interlinear translation that is used more often. The denotative meaning is used as if taken straight from the dictionary, but the grammar of the TT is respected (16). Communicative translation uses standards from the target language (TL) to express equivalents in the source language (SL), such as idioms (17). On the other end of the spectrum is free translation, which displays extreme TL bias. It aims at only global correspondence between ST and TT textual units (16–17).

Matiu summarizes Lefevere's list of different strategies as

> Phonemic translation (attempts to reproduce the sound of the original in the target language, producing an acceptable paraphrase of the sense); Literal translation (word-for-word translation distorts the original sense and syntax); Metrical translation (concentrates on reproducing the meter); Poetry into prose (distorts the sense, communicative value and syntax of the original); Rhymed translation (the translator enters into a "double bondage" of meter and rhyme, the product being a "caricature" of the original); Blank verse translation (restrictions imposed upon the translator, but greater accuracy and higher degree of literalness); Interpretation (the substance of the original is retained but the form is destroyed).
>
> (128)

In addition to this division, Venuti points out two strategies that I believe are relevant to earlier translations of Arabic poetry. The first is domestication, a descriptive term to make a literary text appear as though it was written in English (19). This involves toning down or erasing culture-specific elements. That is the most dominant mode of translation in the Anglo-American world today (20). The second is foreignization, a prescriptive term to make the reader aware of the text's foreign origin. It refuses to offer a smooth reading experience (20). Both forms are invested in cultural reception of the translated work and can be used to create an effect of exoticization of the ST, for instance, or, in contrast, to normalize it and remove its distinctive cultural features. Relevant to those two strategies are the translator's decision of either transferring the content to the readers or creating a new poem all together (Lefevere 76).

All the above strategies acquire even more significance in the light of division into two main approaches to translation that Connolly makes: a pragmatic approach and a theoretical one. He argues that the pragmatic approach takes into account the dynamic and emotional effect. It is difficult, however, to preserve the impact of the poem while the form remains problematic. He discusses Holmes's distinction between levels or types of translating form, ranging from the Mimetic, where the original form is maintained, the Analogical, where a cultural equivalent is sought, Organic, where the semantic content is allowed to modify the form, and, finally, Deviant, where neither form nor content are represented in the chosen form (174).

Matiu argues that "the main condition for a good translation is a thorough analysis of the source-language text" (132). Connolly is right as he discusses the approach of comparing one or more translations of a poem, "not to make value judgements, but to examine the various strategies employed"

(172). Such comparison can help with the analysis. Indeed, a case in point that illustrates the challenges of translating Arabic poetry is Maisūn bint Baḥdal's poem. The poem was written by Maisūn, wife of Mu'āwiya. She lists the elements of contrast between her new urbanized life in the Umayyad caliph's court and her life as a Bedouin, clearly favoring her former life. The poem is among the few widely translated poems by Arab women of the Umayyad period. Redhouse wrote an article dedicated to studying some of the translations of the poem available at the time. The very fact that the poem was referred to in earlier translations as the "Song of Meysūn" sheds light on its position in an exoticization process of Arabic culture (269). By examining some aspects of the translations within the context of the strategies discussed above, I will try to give an example of the approach adopted in this anthology.

The poem in Arabic goes as follows:

لبيت تخفق الأرواح فيه   أحبّ إلىّ من قصر منيف
ولبس عباءة وتقر عيني   أحب إلي من لبس الشفوف
كسيرة في كسر بيتي   أحب إلي من أكل الرغيف
وأصوات الرياح بكلّ فجّ   أحبّ إليّ من نقر الدفوف
وكلب ينبح الطرّاق عنّي   أحبّ إليّ من قطّ أليف
وبكر يتبع الأظعان صعب   أحبُ إليّ من بعل زفوف
وخرق من بني عمي نحيف   أحبُ إليّ من علج علوف
خشونة عيشتي في البدو أشهى   إلى نفسي من العيش الطريف
فما أبغي سوى وطني بديلًا   فحسبي ذاك من وطن شريف
(Al-Udhari 79)

It is important to keep in mind that there were slight variations among versions of the poem, where بني عمي نحيف is بني عمّي ثقيف which would substitute "thin" or "skinny" with "skillful" or "clever," although the thin version makes more sense as it stands in contrast to fattened or well-fed donkey, especially that the entire poem is contrasting two lifestyles. It also suits the word خرق more as it implies weak-boned, a weakling, foolish, or even unskillful.

My attempt to translate the poem is the following,

A house throbbing with people
Is more pleasing to me than a lavish palace.

A dog that barks to drive wanderers away from me
Is more pleasing to me than a tame cat.

Wearing a cloak and being content
Is more pleasing to me than wearing sheer clothes.

Eating a small crumb in a corner in my home
Is more pleasing to me than eating a loaf.

The sound of the wind in every path
Is more pleasing to me to than the strumming tambourines.

A difficult calf that follows howdahs,
Is more pleasing to me than a fast mule.

Among my cousins a weak and slender-built one
Is more pleasing to me than an overfed ass.

My rough life among the Bedouins
Is sweeter to me than soft living.

For all I want is my homeland instead
Suffice it to say for me that it is a land of honor.

In the translation I attempted, I gave priority to the message as a whole, as well as the meaning of individual words and metaphors. I had to sacrifice rhyme scheme as it would have necessitated the choice of words that are not related to the original text, especially given the length of the poem and the very controlled structure of parallel contrasts that, I believe, is more important to conveying the meaning than rhyme. For instance, I considered using the word "feline" for cat and "fine" for "sheer clothes" to add rhyme, but chose not to since "sheer" is closer to شفوف (literally transparent), especially given that the poet might be insinuating her disdain for the loose dress codes of the court.

Among the early translations cited by Redhouse is Joseph Carlyle's:

The russet suit of camel's hair,
With spirits light and eye serene,

Is dearer to my bosom far,
Than all the trappings of a queen.

The humble tent, and murmuring breeze,
That whistles through its fluttering walls,

My unaspiring fancy please,
Better than towers and splendid halls.

Th' attendant colts, that bounding fly,
And frolic by tho litter's side,

Are dearer in Maisuna's eye,
Than gorgeous mules in all their pride.

The watch-dog's voice, that bays whene'er
A stranger seeks his master's cot,

Sounds sweeter in Maisuna's ear,
Than yonder trumpet's long-drawn note.

The rustic youth, unspoiled by art,
Son of my kindred, poor but free,

Will ever to Maisuna's heart,
Be dearer, pampered fool, than thee.
(269)

Another one is Richard Burton's,

O take those purple robes away,
Give back my cloak of camel's hair,
And bear me from this tow'ring pile
To where the Black Tents flap i' the air.
The camel's colt with falt'ring trend,
The dog that bays at all but me,
Delight me more than ambling mules
Than every art of minstrelsy.
And any cousin, poor but free,
Might take me, fatted ass! from thee.
(269–70)

The third one is by Alice M. Frere, cited by Redhouse as Mrs. Godfrey Clerk,

1 A hut that the winds make tremble
Is dearer to me than a noble palace;
2 And a dish of crumbs on the floor of my home
Is dearer to me than a varied feast;
3 And the soughing of the breeze through every crevice
Is dearer to me than the beating of drums;

4 And a camel's wool abah which gladdens my eye
Is dearer to me than filmy robes;
5 And a dog barking around my path
Is dearer to me than a coaxing cat;
6 And a restive young camel, following tho litter,
Is dearer to me than a pacing mule;
7 And a feeble boor from midst my cousinhood,
Is dearer to me than a rampant ass.

(271)

The fourth is Gibb's translation, titled, "*Meysun's Ditty*":

To dress in camlet smock with cool and placid eyne,
Were liefer far to me than robes of gauze to wear;
A tent, wherethrough the winds in gentle wafts should breathe,
Were liefer far to me than palace haught and fair;
A wayward camel-colt behind tho litter-train,
Were liefer far to me than hinny debonair;
A dog that bayed tho guests ere yet they came me nigh,
Were liefer far to me than cat with fondling air;
To eat a scantling meal aside within the tent,
Were liefer far to me than feast on dainties rare;
The soughing moan of winds that blow through every glen,
Were liefer far to me than sounding tabors' blare;
A slim but generous youth from 'mong my uncle's sons,
Were liefer far to me than foddered ass, I swear.

(274)

A different translation is posted on the Hill Museum & Manuscript Library blog:

Aye, dearer to me is a tent where the winds roar than a lofty palace.
Dearer to me is a rough woolen cloak with a happy heart than clothes of well-spun wool.
Dearer to me is a morsel of food at the side of the tent than a cake to eat.
Dearer to me are the sounds of winds in every mountain path than the tap of the tambourine.
Dearer to me is a young, unyielding camel following a litter than an active mule.
And dearer to me is a thin generous man from among my cousins than a strong lavishly fed man.

(Adamcmccollum)

The previous attempts display instances of Venuti's notion of foreignization. The insertion of a cloak made of camel hair in these several translations is an example of forcing foreignization on the original. There is no camel hair anywhere in the poem. The same goes for tents with an added adjective of a black tent in Burton's poem. Again, there are no tents in the poem. The word بيت means home, and as a matter of fact might imply a house more than a tent, and, even if it does not, then the type of home referred to in the poem is clearly not determined. Carlyle implies a house as he uses the word "walls." It is difficult not to see the use of tents and camel's hair for Maisūn's cloak as examples of foreignization.

There is an example of domestication in some of the translations as well. Describing the cousin that the speaker favors to the caliph as "free," "rustic . . . unspoiled by art," and "poor but free," depends on different versions of the original that describe the cousin in one version as فقير (poor), in another as نحيف (skinny) and in a third one as ثقيف (skillful) (Redhouse 269). Nevertheless, none of them describe the cousin as free. Using that is an overreading of the text from the translator's perspective, to justify that Maisūn prefers a cousin because he is free. As a matter of fact, it is just as likely that the next line might offer a justification, as she describes her hometown as a home of honor, شريف. It might make more sense that honor is the reason she prefers a cousin from her homeland to a caliph used to a politicized court life, which is stereotypically not thought of as honest, rather than freedom, especially that she does not specify freedom as her reason for that preference. Combining both foreignization and domestication in the same translation is not uncommon.

Venuti writes that foreignization and domestication are often seen "as an either/or scenario, when in fact each of the two methods encompasses a range of possible strategies and may in fact co-exist with a given text" (168). Indeed, a relatively more confusing translation is that of أظعان as litter, although it means caravan or howdah. The previous translations seem to be reproducing an image of campsite poetry and tracing the litter of animals after they left a camp. In that case, this is foreignization. On the other hand, it is possible that such translation would be more an instance of domestication, describing the calf as traditional cattle following the litter and giving those tending them a hard time.

In addition to foreignization, the poems display a free translation strategy that allows changes in favor of versification. For instance, the dog barking at strangers in the original poem is extended in Carlyle's poem to "The watchdog's voice, that hays whene'er A stranger seeks his master's cot, Sounds sweeter in Maisuna's ear, Than yonder trumpet's long-drawn note" (Redhouse 269). The product here, although an example of free translation, does not alter the meaning or the intended message of the original.

According to Holmes, analogical translation is among the cultural strategies. It brings a cultural form corresponding to the original. A mimetic strategy maintains the original form (25). All the poems, except Clerk's, attempt a balance between analogical and mimetic, leaning towards the analogical. They acknowledge the existence of halved-lines but present them as couplets. In addition, Carlyle, in particular, maintains a rhyme scheme, in alternating rhyme not couplets, which creates a sense of musicality that echoes the rhyming and rhythmic original, even if using a different rhyme scheme. In maintaining the rhyme scheme and musicality, translators sometimes sacrifice the meaning of the source poem.

A very different translation from the previous attempts is al-Udhari's translation. In the introduction to what I consider his groundbreaking effort to translate classical poetry by Arab women, he clarifies that his approach is intended to express the different climates under which the poems were written. He refers to his translations as "voice copies" that flow in "paralines (paragraph lines)" (22). Al-Udhari's translation for Maisūn's poem is as follows,

1 I'd rather be in a lifethrobbing house than in a tall place.
2 I'd rather have a dog calling lost travellers to my home than a pussycat.
3 I'd have a pleasing smock than a chiffon dress.
4 I'd rather have breadcrumbs in my own house than a whole loaf in a palace.
5 I'd rather listen to the winds voicing through wallcracks than to the sound of tambourines.
6 I'd rather be in the company of my proud and finefigured cousin than with the bloated foreign mass.
7 My simple country life appeals to me more than this soft living.
8 All I want is to be in my country home, indeed it is a noble home.

(78)

I would like to draw a closer comparison of some choices I made that differ from al-Udhari's. His strategy is much closer to literal translation as far as meaning is concerned and a free translation as far as form is concerned. The translation does not add exoticizing cultural assumptions such as camel hair and wool. Mughazy defines substitution as a translation strategy that is useful when no ideal equivalent is available (30). This strategy is dependent on the function of the source word, rather than just its meaning (32). Al-Udhari uses substitution in translating the dog barking in the poem, which I agree is the most adequate strategy to use for this line. However, it misinterprets a key word here. "I'd rather have a dog calling travelers to my home" is the opposite of the sentence in Arabic as the dog barks at passersby and drives them away. In the expression ينبح الطرّاق عنّي *yanbaḥu ʿannī* means literally "barks those in the road away from me" as the عن *ʿann* following a verb denotes separation not proximity, such as in رغب عن *raghiba ʿann* which means to no longer want or to not want, as opposed to the same verb رغب *raghiba* if followed by the preposition في *fī* in رغب في which denotes to want or desire. The verb نبح عن is similar to زاد عن *zāda ʿann* which means to defend, in the sense of drive away attackers.

Naturally, some of the choices made in translation are harder than others. Mughazy explains morphological unpacking as a translation strategy that is useful in translating morphologically complex words (37). In this poem, one example is translating the word فجّ. Al-Udhari translates it as "wallcracks." It can make sense to see the metaphor as wind blowing through cracks in the wall. Nevertheless, the word فجّ does mean a wide path or terrain, and, where it means an opening in a concrete structure it usually implies one bigger than a crack in a wall. It would, in that case, usually imply a path dug in a mountain. Moreover, the second half of the line that describes the alternate palace life refers to the sounds of tambourines. Therefore, I chose to visualize both metaphors as a critique of the streets and roads of both locations, one filled with noisy processions with tambourines, and the other with winds traveling in the natural terrain of pathways.

Some choices are also based on an attempt to preserve a sense of musicality whenever possible, without sacrificing meaning or intent. An example of choices I made in that respect is translating كِسر. Al-Udhari translates كسر بيتي as "my own house." It specifically refers to a corner or part of a house. While "my own house" does deliver the message and the emotional impact of ownership that the speaker highlights, I felt that literally translating كسر into "a corner in my home" would both impart the sense of ownership while preserving the specific details that even a corner in the speaker's home is preferable for her. In addition, in my translation the consonance of the k sound in crumb and corner echoes that of the k sound in كسيرة and كسر.

Lefevere expresses a key challenge with translating Arabic poetry in general, "The problem is that of single end rhyme. Every bayt [line in a poem] in the qasidah [Arabic poetic form, closer to ode] ends in the same sound. No translator in English has ever tried to keep it" (64). I chose to leave the Maisūn poem rhymeless mainly because I prioritized the accuracy of word choice and meaning over musicality. There were times that I was more fortunate, however, and, perhaps better inspired, to maintain all three. A poem by Bint al-Ḥubāb goes,

أقول لعمرو والسياط تلفني　　لهنّ على متني شرّ دليل
فإشهد يا غيران أني أحبّه　　بسوطك فاضربني وأنت ذليلي
(Al-Udhari 89)

In this poem Bint al-Ḥubāb addresses her husband, ʿAmr, who whips her because she is in love with another man. The literal translation of the poem, without versification, is:

> I tell ʿAmr as the whips circle me, they are on my body the evilest evidence. So bear witness, you jealous one, that I love him. With your whip beat me and you are the one humiliated by me.

Once again, the only translation I found for that poem was al-Udhari's,

> 1 Why you are raving mad, husband, just because I love another man?
> 2 Go on, whip me, every scar on my body will show the pain I cause you.
> (87)

Al-Udhari's translation adds information not revealed in the poem. There is no mention in the two lines of the source poem that ʿAmr is the speaker's husband. The translation removes ʿAmr altogether and refers to him as the husband. There is also no mention of ʿAmr's anger in the source poem, whereas the translation describes him as "raving mad." The entire phrase of "just because I love another man" explains the situation to the reader but does not transfer the emotional impact on the two characters in the poem, ʿAmr and the speaker. It is important to point out my understanding of the role of supplying additional information in translation. Mughazy refers to this practice in the context of translation of paraphrasing. He argues that additional information can help readers "recognize the referents of the source words in the absence of direct equivalents" (38). As paraphrasing can solve problems such as ambiguity and cultural connotations, for instance, Mughazy does not see paraphrasing as a translation strategy of last resort, a position that I agree with fully (39). My critique of the above translation of Bint al-Ḥubāb's poem is not a statement against paraphrasing or using additional information in translation. My criticism is based on the fact that additional information does not provide, in my opinion, a better understanding of this particular text. It only detracts from the spontaneity of a poem which was written by a woman addressing a man who already knows the context of the poem. Part of the impact of the poem is the husband's familiarity with his wife's relationship with her lover, which reverses the humiliation he is trying to inflict on her. Explaining that in the translation will make it seem as if she is explaining it to him, thus reducing the impact of the burdensome shared knowledge that created such tension between them in the first place.

In addition to trying to preserve the rhyme, I left out additional information not in the Arabic poem such as "my husband," and "because I love another man," as well as words not used in the poem such as "scars," while keeping words that I believe are central to the poem, such as "jealous" and "humiliated." My attempt goes as follows,

> I tell ʿAmr as the whip circles around my body,
> Lashes are the most wicked proof it's true.
>
> So bear witness, you who are jealous, that I love him.
> Flog me, but the one who is humiliated is you.

Another poem I can use here to illustrate the use of rhyme is Umm al-Ward al-ʿAjlāniyya's poem:

> إن تسألوني عنه ما كان الخبر   عذّبني الشيخ بأنواع السَّحر
> حتّى إذا ما كان في وقت السَّحر   وركّب المفتاح في القفل انكسر
> ورعدت فقحته بلا مطر.
>
> (Al-Udhari 91)

A literal explanatory translation of this erotic invective is:

> If you ask me what was the news, the old man tormented me with all kinds of staying up late, until it was pre-dawn, and he put the key in the lock, it broke, and his little twig thundered with no rain.

Al-Udhari translated this poem and preserved the meaning as,

> 1. If you want to know how this old man fared with me, this is what went on.
> 2. He lolled me the whole night through, and when dawn flashed his private lips thundered rainlessly and his key wilted in my lock.
>
> (90)

And my attempt to preserve the rhyme goes as follows,

> If you want to know how that night prevailed,
> The old man teased me again and again,
> Until the time before dawn, and then
> When he put the key in the lock, it failed.
> And when his twig thundered, there was no rain.

In preserving the rhyme, I simultaneously attempted not to sacrifice the metaphor and the intended meaning of the source text. If I had to make that choice, I would have prioritized the meaning over the rhyme scheme.

An additional strategy of translation that I try to avoid but resort to in rare occasions is transliteration, reproducing the sound of a word in the SL using the letters of the TL, a strategy most commonly used with proper nouns. According to Mughazy, transliteration amounts to lexical borrowing to fill a lexical gap (40–1), and, as such, in this book I limit my use of transliteration to names. The main exceptions are the words *jāriyat* (the slave girl or concubine of), *zawjat* (the wife of), *ibn/bin* (the son of), *ibnat/bint* (the daughter of), *ghazal* (love poetry), *ghazal ʿafīf* (non-explicit love poetry), *ghazal ṣarīḥ* (sexually explicit love poetry), *majlis* (assembly, used in the context of this book to refer to a literary salon), and *ijāza*. The last word, *ijāza*, is not that simple. *Ijāza* is used in the context of this book to refer to a common poetic practice in classical Arabic poetry. It is a poetry challenge. The challenger would recite a few lines of verse and ask a poet to finish them, using the same meter and rhyme. This challenge was so common in the world of this book that it was natural for a poet walking down the street who runs into another poet to randomly challenge her or him to an *ijāza*, to finish a poem. This form of impromptu poetry is a measure of the virtuosity and talent of the poets of the age, as well as an indication of the joy poetry brought, and the esteem poets enjoyed. In this book, I use the translation system outlined by the *International Journal of Middle East Studies.*

I agree with Lefevere that "Both metrical padding and highly explanatory prose tend to dilute the power of the primordial feature of the early qasidahs" (64). In this anthology, I try to maintain the difficult balance in the scale of faithfulness to text set by Dickins, Hervey, and Higgins, where on one end is Literal translation, followed by approaches that they describe as Faithful, with the middle stance as Balanced translation, then moving on to an Idiomatic approach, and, finally, on the other end, Free (17). But, then, again, in the arduous task of translating poetry, the aim of the translator is significant. As Connolly puts it, "Evaluation must, however, also be based on the translator's aims. A translation has to be judged in terms of its consistency with these aims and not on something it was never to be" (175). Mine is to balance content and form, making every effort to maintain a reasonable resemblance to the content, especially the musicality of the original, but decisively prioritizing content and leaning towards it when that balance eludes me, while also paying special attention to communicating as much as possible the psychological and cultural impact of the original.

Bibliography

Adamcmccollum. "The Dearness of Home: Arabic Verse Attributed to Maysūn Bint Baḥdal al-Kalbiyya." *Hmmlorientallia*, 19 Sep. 2014, hmmlorientalia.wordpress.com/2014/09/19/the-dearness-of-home-arabic-verse-attributed-to-maysun-bint-ba%E1%B8%A5dal-al-kalbiyya/. Accessed 9 Dec. 2017.

Al-Aṣfahānī, Abū-l-faraj. *Kitāb al-Aghānī*. Edited by Iḥsān ʿAbbās, Ibrāhīm as-Saʿāfīn and Bakr ʿAbbās, Beirut: Dār Ṣādir, 2008.

———. *Al-Imāʾ ash-Shawāʿir*. Edited by Jalīl al-ʿAṭiyya, Beirut: Dār an-Niḍāl, 1984.

Al-Udhari, Abdullah. *Classical Poetry by Arab Women: A Bilingual Anthology*. Beirut: Saqi Books, 1999.

Bassnett, Susan and André Lefevere. *Constructing Cultures: Essays on Literary Translation*. UK: Multilingual Matters, 1998.

Connolly, David. "Poetry Translation." *The Routledge Encyclopedia of Translation Studies*, edited by Mona Baker, Abingdon, UK: Routledge, 1998, pp. 170–5.

Dickins, James, Sándor Hervey and Ian Higgins. *Thinking Arabic Translation: A Course in Translation Method: Arabic to English*. Abingdon, UK: Routledge, 2002.

Holmes, James. *Translated!: Papers on Literary Translation and Translation Studies*. Amsterdam: Brill Rodopi, 1988.

IJMES Translation and Transliteration Guide. *International Journal of Middle East Studies*, 2013, www.ijmes.chass.ncsu.edu/ijmes_translation_and_transliteration_guide.htm

Jakobson, Roman. "On Linguistic Aspects of Translation." *On Translation*, edited by Reuben Brower, Cambridge, MA: Harvard UP, 1959, pp. 232–9.

Lefevere, André. "Acculturating Bertolt Brecht." *Constructing Cultures: Essays on Literary Translation*, edited by Susan Bassnett and André Lefevere, UK: Multilingual Matters, 1998, pp. 109–22.

Matiu, Ovidiu. "Translating Poetry: Contemporary Theory and Hypotheses." *The 5th International Conference of Professional Communication and Translation Studies,13–14 Sep. 2007 Timisoara, Romania*, edited by Rodica Superceanu and Daniel Dejica, Department of Communication and Foreign Languages, Timisoara: Politehnica University of Timisoara, 2008.

Mihanā, ʿAbdu-l-Amīr, editor. *Akhbār an-Nisāʾ fī Kitāb al-Aghānī l-Abī-l-faraj al-Aṣfahānī*. Beirut: Muʾassasat al-Kutub ath-Thaqāfiyya, 1996.

Mughazy, Mustafa. *The Georgetown Guide to Arabic-English Translation*. Washington DC: Georgetown UP, 2016.

Redhouse, James W. "Observations on the Various Texts and Translations of the So-Called 'Song of Meysūn': An Inquiry into Meysūn's Claim to Its Authorship; and an Appendix on Arabic Transliteration and Pronunciation." New Series of *The Journal of the Royal Asiatic Society of Great Britain and Ireland*, vol. 18, no. 2, Apr., 1886, pp. 268–322.

Venuti, Lawrence. *The Translator's Invisibility*. Abingdon, UK: Routledge, 2008.

2 Poets of the pre-Islamic period

1. ʿAbla bint Khālid at-Tamīmiyya

She was married to a man from the Jashm clan. It is said that he gave her lard to sell in the ʿUkāẓ market and sent his nephew with her. She sold not only the lard, but the mules carrying it, and bought wine with the money. When she ran out of wine and money, she sold her husband's nephew and ran away. She recited the following poem,

I gave my ride and what is on it for a goblet,
Woe to me, this goblet will be my undoing.
I exchanged his nephew for pleasure,
And feared no blame from those who would chastise.

2. Ad-Daʿjāʾ bint Wahb

Her brother Al-Muntashir fought frequently in raids against Banī al-Ḥārith. He remained undefeated in battle until, one day, he was ambushed and killed. In the following poem she described how she sensed her brother's death before he was killed,

I have received words that do not please me,
Words neither of wonder nor of scorn.
Since I have heard them I have been forlorn,
I would warn him if of any use warning could ever be.

3. Al-Basūs bint Munqidh al-Bikriyya

One of the fiercest and longest recorded wars on the pre-Islamic Arab peninsula, the Basūs war started when cattle that belonged to al-Basūs bint Munqidh al-Taimiyya grazed the pasture of Kulaib ibn Rabīʿa al-Taghlibī, who killed the cattle. As a result, al-Basūs wrote a eulogy for her cattle, shaming her tribe into avenging her honor. Her nephew al-Jassās ibn Murra al-Shaibānī responded and killed Kulaib, thus starting the war that lasted for at least two decades, possibly four, from CE 494.

> If I were sheltered by someone who would rescue me,
> Sa'd would not be slighted as long as my neighbor he would be.
> But I am in a house of estrangement,
> Where a wolf, when it chooses to attack, would attack sheep that
> belonged to me.

4. Al-Fāri'a bint Mu'āwiya al-Qushairiyya

She wrote a poem gloating over Banī Kilāb who had several men and women taken as captives in a battle. Her poem is an example of the lesser known genre of poetry of gloating,

> God has healed my heart and avenged me from a people
> That wasted Qudāma on the day of Nisār,
> They wasted a boy who was not lazy,
> A boy who rode danger daringly,
> And whose raids would go far.
> His spear drove away steeds
> With stabs like fire from the nostrils of mares.
> Dogs scatter away from Ja'far, before the morning stares.

5. Al-Jaidā' bint Zāhir al-Zubaidiyya

Her husband Khālid ibn Muḥārib al-Zubaidī was killed by the famous warrior slave poet 'Antara in Ḥijāz. She wrote this eulogy for her husband,

> O my people, my cheeks are scorched by tears,
> My calamity is immense and sleep has deserted me.
> I had a knight who from the cup of death was fed
> By the hands of a slave from Banī 'abs in hostility,
> A full moon he was, but to earth he fell
> When arrows struck him from the hands of a slave.

6. Al-Khansā' bint Zuhair bin Abī Sulmā

She was the daughter of Zuhair bin Abī Sulmā, one of the great seven pre-Islamic poets who wrote the mu'allaqāt, or hanging poems. She wrote in a eulogy of her father,

My longing spares me nothing. Neither would an omen or a spell,
If one meets one's end, one is led where the warnings befell.

7. An-Nawwār al-Jul

She was married to Mālik ibn Zaid ibn Tamīm. On their wedding night, his brother Saʿd took their cattle to graze but did not do a good job. When Mālik reproached him, Saʿd's excuse was that the cattle did not want to graze and he recited the following lines,

The day they were supposed to be led to water,
They remained yellow, treading on grass.

When Mālik told an-Nawwār his brother's excuse, she told him to tell his brother the following lines, that were later on often cited to describe a job done poorly,

Saʿd took the cattle away
And hiked his clothes up first.
O Saʿd, this is not the way,
To quench the cattle's thirst.

8. Asmāʾ al-Mariyya

She was a sex worker in ʿukāẓ. In some accounts she is held responsible for the death of Muʿawiya, one of al-Khansāʾ's brothers. Muʿawiya met Asmāʾ and wanted her to follow him, but she told him she belonged to the "master of Arabs," Hāshim ibn Ḥarmala. As a result, Muʿawiya attempted to raid Hāshim's people, but Hāshim and his brother Duraid ambushed Muʿawiya and killed him. This incident started more raids and battles that involved Ṣakhr, al-Khansāʾ's brother who would become the main subject of her laments later.

Among Asmāʾ's surviving poetry is the following,

O you two mountains of Nuʿmān, by God let the breeze of love pass through,
For love is a wind, if breathed by a broken heart it cleansed it where it blew.

9. As-Sulaka Umm as-Sulaik

She was the mother of as-Sulaik. Her name and his are probably derived from the Arabic verb *salaka*, which means to walk in a path or to find one's way, thus referring to the family profession as guides and trackers. As a tracker, as-Sulaik had a reputation of being faster than a horse. He knew how to trace caravans and horses in the desert and was a well-known guide. He was also known as a hired warrior. With no clan to protect him, as-Sulaik was a poet and outlaw on the fringe of community. He raided Yemeni tribes for ʿAbdu-l-Malik ibn Muwailik al-Khuthʿamī in return for protection, which apparently did not last forever. One day as as-Sulaik was returning from a raid on Yemen, he passed by a small house in Khuthʿam, asking for directions. He had sex with the daughter of the house, and when the hosts found out they tracked him and killed him, ending his legendary ability to remain untraceable. His mother as-Sulaka wrote the following eulogy for him,

He went around seeking high ground
Away from death, so he died.
I wish my verse was misled,
What has killed you?
Were you ill and did not return,
Or did an enemy take you by surprise?
Anything can do you in,
When your time comes.
Death tracks down a fellow
Wherever he treks.

10. Bārra bint ʿAbdu-l-Muṭṭalib

One of the daughters of ʿAbdu-l-Muṭṭalib, Muḥammad's grandfather. It is said that when he was on his deathbed, he asked his daughters to gather around him and asked each one of them to tell him what eulogy she would say after he died. His daughters were Ṣafīyya, Bārra, ʿĀtika, Umm Ḥakīm, Arwā, and Umaima. One by one, they read him their poems. This is Bārra's poem,

My eyes, generous with flowing tears you should be,
For he who holds the glory of noble origins and generosity,
And holds the glory of status and success,
With beautiful features and an honor so great.
His generosity inspires gratitude in old age,
His honor and dignity instill pride.
He is known for patience and kindness in duress.
His reasons to be proud are too numerous to address.
His deeds are a debt his people shall hold,
Like the hovering light of the moon.
Death has come for him,
But his deeds it could not smite

With the distractions of fate
And the calamities of the night.

11. Ḍāḥiya al-Hilāliyya

A Yemeni poet who was known for love poetry,

I intend to walk in the righteous path
Then love pulls me away from the path and I follow.
It is not like passion is a prisoner in Ṣanʿāʾ
With its feet tied to Prince Kabūl.

In another poem, she wrote,

I hope as my soul lives in hope,
To spend my night with a Yemeni lover.

12. Dahknatūs bint Luqaiṭ

She was the daughter of Luqaiṭ ibn Zurāra from the Tamīm clan. It was said that her father was on good terms with Persians and named her after a Persian princess. Her clan was in war with ʿAbs and ʿĀmir clans. She used to accompany her father to battle. During a battle known as Shaʿb Jibla, her father and his men came across a man of high status called Karb ibn Ṣafwān ibn al-ḥubāb as-Saʿdī. Luqaiṭ asked Karb whether Karb would tell the ʿAbs and ʿĀmir clans that Tamīm's army was advancing. Karb gave Luqaiṭ his word that he would not tell anyone. Dahknatūs did not believe Karb and advised her father against letting Karb go. Her father did not heed her warning and sent her home. As his army progressed, however, they were met by ʿAbs, who were warned by Karb. Her father was among the captives. He was beaten to death by his captors. When she learned of her father's death, Dahknatūs wrote the following poem,

O calamities, woe upon the ones who struck
Luqaiṭ among the clan of ʿAbs
For they have smeared a face covered with honor
But killers are deaf to the one they kill.

13. Dijāja bint Ṣafwān

Her mother was also a poet. When her mother was ridiculed by rival poets, Dijāja wrote the following in her defense,

We tell them what Quṭām has said before,
For every people must have a leader.
The honor of the children of Sa'd is to devour
And stop their rivals in the marketplace.

14. Fāṭima bint Murr al-Khuthʿamiyya

She was a pagan priestess and a contemporary of ʿAbdullah, Muḥammad's father. She offered to marry him but he married Āmina bint Wahb, Muḥammad's mother. She recited the following poem about that,

Not everything a man gets, he gets by taking action,
Nor is it that all he loses, he loses by inaction.
Now that Āmina has what she had from him,
She must have had an honor that is second to none.

15. Fāriʿa al-Muriyya

She was the daughter of Shaddād ibn al-Murī. Her brother Masʿūd ibn Shaddād ibn al-Murī was captured by the Sahm clan during a war between his clan and the Murra clan. They did not recognize him at first but when they did, they killed him. She heard that he was thirsty and asked for water before his death, but they denied him water and killed him. She recited the following poem for him,

He is the youth whose neighbors praise his sight in winter,
They put his fire down.
They stabbed him the treacherous stabbing,
And followed it leaving him to gurgle in thirst.

16. Hazīla al-Judaisiyya

Her husband divorced her and wanted to take their son from her. They went to ʿImlīq, the ʿĀdait king. ʿImlīq ruled that neither of them should have the child and that he was going to take him among his slaves. She recited in response,

We have sought our brother from the tribe of Ṭasm for his judgment,
Then his verdict for Hazīla was unjust.
For the life of me, you have judged impiously,
And knew not what you were judging.
I regret this and I have not regretted my initial ill fortune,
And my husband has become regretful with this verdict.

When he heard her poem, ʿImlīq was so furious he sold her and her husband into slavery, and gave each one of them a portion of the other's price. Ṭasm is one of the early tribes that were contemporaries of the ʿĀd tribes, normally referred to as Extinct Arabs, *al-ʿĀrab al-Bāʾida.*

17. Hind al-Julāḥiyya

She is from the ʿĀmir clan. ʿUmair ibn al-Ḥubāb raided the Kalb clan and killed many of its members. Hind recited the following poem to motivate the warriors of Kalb,

> Is there going to be revenge for the blood
> Of a people attacked by ʿUmair ibn al-Ḥubāb?
> Would one day someone from ʿĀmir refuse to yield,
> Someone who is alive and feels the shame,
> A worshipper of Wad or someone nearby?
> If they do not avenge themselves for what they suffered,
> They would become slaves of Banī Kilāb.
> After living among Banī al-Julāḥ,
> And after those you left buried in the sand,
> Would a dignified man among you accept life?
> No life there is for those living in defeat.

18. Hind bint al-Khus

Hind had a disagreement with her sister Khumʿa. They went to Qulmus, a judge and a sage, and she recited a poem in his praise,

> If God rewards those who are gracious with loyalty,
> May He reward you Qulmus on my behalf with generosity.

It is said that she once saw a dove fly by to join other doves. She counted 66 doves and recited,

> I wish a dove like this was ours,
> And half more with him,
> Added to the doves of our people,
> We then would have a hundred.

19. Ḥusaina bint Jābir bint Bujair al-ʿIjlī

Al-Ḥārith ibn Tawlab captured Ḥusaina during a raid by the ʿAbd Manāt clan on the ʿIjl and Ḥanīfa clans. Ḥusaina's brother was Abjar ibn Jābir al-ʿIjlī from the ʿIjl clan and she was the bride of Tammām from the Ḥanīfa clan. As the story goes, Tammām went to negotiate her release but she herself refused to return with him, shaming him for failing to protect her. She only agreed to leave when her brother Abjar came and paid al-Ḥārith to set her free. She recited this poem shaming Tammām,

Tammām, you left me to their spears,
And in the scattered dust ran away.
Then blame me for not returning to you,
For that is the last thing that I will do.
I have found your women on the meeting day
Are placed on the lines ahead of you.

20. Ibnat aḍ-Ḍaḥāk bin Sufyān (Ḥabība bint aḍ-Ḍaḥāk)

She was one of the wives of ʿAbbās ibn Mirdās. He spent the night with her before starting the journey to Medina to join Muḥammad there. When she found out he was planning on supporting Muḥammad and his followers, she was furious. She packed and went back to her clan of Ibn Sufyān as-Salmī. She wrote of ʿAbbās's decision,

Hasn't ʿAbbās ibn Mirdās been warned by my vision of people in distress,
Approached by supporters of the most brave and generous of men,
Who protect their people from all duress?
For the life of me, if you follow Muḥammad's faith then,
And abandon your brothers of great purity and deeds,
The dignity of this soul you shall replace,
The day you switch the sharp blades, with disgrace,
Of a people who in war, rhetoric, and hospitality leads,
Whose swords would turn dishonor to grace,
And whose enemies at war are pierced by their steeds.

21. Jalīla bint Murra ash-Shaibāniyya

Her brother al-Jassās ibn Murra killed her husband Kulaib during the Basūs war. When she left and stayed with her clan, she found out that her sister-in-law described her leaving as "the departure of aggression and the parting of gloating," accusing Jalīla of complicity with al-Jassās in murdering Kulaib. In response, Jalīla wrote,

O daughter of my people, if blame must be made,
Ask first and haste not to chide.

Once the bearer of the blame you decide,
Then you can cast your blame and your tirade.

22. Jāriyat Humām ibn Murra

She was from the people of Dhahl bin Shaibān and was one of the slaves of Humām ibn Murra. He killed her when he heard her recite the following erotic poem,

O Humām ibn Murra, my heart yearns
For that which men have.

O Humām ibn Murra, my heart yearns
For a bald head near sprouting hair.

O Humām ibn Murra, my heart yearns
For a hard branch to fill my source of urine.

23. Karma bint Ḍilʿ

She was the mother of Mālik ibn Zaid, one of the warriors of the Bakr clan. She was known for leading women into battle singing her poems to motivate warriors.

We are the daughters of the shining star,
We walk on soft pillows,
Like flying doves,
With musk in our hair,
Pearls on our necks,
When you return,
We shall embrace you.

24. Lailā al-ʿAfīfa

She was Lailā bint Lukaiz ibn Murra ibn Asad, from the Nizār clan. A Persian prince abducted her and took her to Persia. He wanted to marry her but she would not let him touch her. That earned her the title al-ʿAfīfa which means the chaste one. Her fiancé, al-Barrāq ibn Rawḥān rode to Persia to save her. They returned and got married. Her story is cited as an example of Arab-Persian rivalry and is used to glorify the Arab side highlighting qualities such as chastity for women and strength for men. Her poem calling for al-Barrāq to come to her rescue is cited in situations of distress,

I wish al-Barrāq had an eye to see,
What befell me of suffering and plight.
O Wā'il and 'Uqail, woe unto you little soldiers,
With weeping help me.
Your sister was tortured, woe upon you
Tortured by neglect day and night.
The foreigner lies he has not come near me,
I still have some remnants of modesty by my side.
Shackle me, torture me, do to me all atrocities as you might,
For I hate your desire, and by sweet death I prefer to abide.

25. Lailā bint Mirdās

She was married to Sālim ibn Quḥāfa al-'Anbarī from the Qaḥfān clan. Once her brother visited them and Sālim gave him a camel and asked Lailā for a rope to tie the camel with. He then gave her brother another camel and then another, asking her for a rope each time. She told him eventually she had no ropes left, then gave him a shawl or scarf she had to use as a rope and recited,

You swore an oath, Ibn Qaḥfān,
By He who provides in mountains and in the plains,
There are still many ropes I can count,
By which the camels can tread,
So give whoever comes asking and do not be miserly.
I have enough reins for the camels
And there is no excuse that you have.

26. Manfūsa bint Zaid al-Khail

She was married to Duraid ibn al-Ṣamma. She has a well-known poem that she used to recite while playing with her son,

You who look like my brother, look like your father.
As for my father, you will not have that,
For your hands are too short to reach him.

27. Raiṭa bint 'Āṣiyya

Her brother 'Amr ibn 'Āṣiyya was raiding the Hudhail with a group of men. A woman in a house on the road saw them and told her son to go warn the Hudhail clan. When 'Amr and his men reached a mountain overlooking the Hudhail clan, he noticed that they were preparing for battle and understood that they had been warned. While waiting for the right moment to attack, ʿAmr and his men ran out of water. He asked his companions if any of them would volunteer to go down to the water well, but none of them agreed. ʿAmr went by himself and was ambushed by an old man and two young men. He managed to kill the old man but was captured by the two men. He asked them to let him drink water before killing him, but they refused and killed him without quenching his thirst. Raiṭa wrote the following poem about his gruesome death,

Ibn ʿĀṣiyya who was killed among you
Has left me in a mountain road that he once protected.
The vast difficult terrain feared him,
Even the cattle did not approach its plants.

28. Rayṭa bint Jadhl aṭ-Ṭaʿān

Her husband Rabīʿa ibn Makdim from the Kināna clan was killed in battle during a raid known as the Day of Dhaʿīna by her clan Kināna on the Jashm clan. However, before he was killed, he broke his spear and Duraid ibn aṣ-Ṣumma, a man from the enemy Jashm, saved his life and spared him. Later, Duraid was captured by Kināna. While in captivity, a woman from Kināna saw him and told everyone the story of how he saved one of their clan. They decided that Duraid's fate should be decided by Rabīʿa's wife, Rayṭa, since it was he who was the one that Duraid had saved. Rayṭa agreed to free Duraid and recited,

We shall graciously reward Duraid for Rabīʿa,
For each one for their deeds is paid in kind,
If good they hold,
Then good they shall behold,
If evil, then evil they shall find.
Upon him we shall bestow
Blessings of no small magnitude,
For casting his long spear aside.
His hands have earned him our gratitude,
For he who blesses,
Blessings by him abide.

29. Ṣafiyya al-Bāhiliyya

Her eulogy for her brother is well known,

We were like two branches in the sand around a bush,
Blossomed for a while promising to reach the best that trees can offer,

Until it was said that our tree has two long branches,
And their fruits are expected.
But the suspicions of time raided my other one,
For time leaves nothing and nothing it spares.
Go with good repute, you went when you were my sight and my hearing.
We were like stars of the night, with a moon between us
That lights the darkness,
Then from its place between us the moon fell.

30. Ṣafiyya bint Thaʿlaba al-Shaibāniyya

She was referred to as the Pilgrim. Hind bint al-Nuʿmān sought refuge with her from Persian armies. Ṣafiyya gave Hind refuge and wrote to entice her people to fight the Persians,

Upon my people of Shaibān and the Arabs I call,
Honored among them I am, and humiliated I shall not be.
Tell the greedy: the young men of war are here with me.
For Khosrow I have hearts and bodies.

In another poem, she wrote,

I am the pilgrim from the best of Wail,
I am the shelter when blood is spilled.
Wail, revolt, for this is your time.
And for every great deed there is a time.

31. Subaiʿa bint al-Aḥab

She was known for poems glorifying Mecca. In the following poem she urges her son Khālid to respect Mecca,

My son, in Mecca do not inflict injustice on young or old.
Protect its sanctity. Let not arrogance taint you much,
For whoever is unjust in Mecca receives the evil touch.

32. Suʿdā al-Asadiyya

Suʿdā and her cousin had one of the earliest stories of ill-fated lovers in Arabic literary history. Her cousin's family wanted him to marry a wealthier bride and her indignant father forced her to marry another man, which broke her cousin's heart. Once, her cousin saw her walking. He recited,

For the life of me, Suʿdā, for a long time I have been without a mate.
My father I have disobeyed. Both I have done for you.
Leaving all living things, wanting none of them but you,
My love not waiting for any of them.

To his lines she replied,

My love, do not rush to understand my reasons,
Suffice it the plight I must undergo and the hardship.
The tears and sighs that overcome me,
Almost make my soul bleed out of love.
I was forced in public,
And could not fight back my family,
By imploring nor by resisting.
But they cannot stop me from dying against their will,
Tomorrow the depth of this cave
Shall be for only me a grave.
Forget not to come tomorrow, and find me,
And forget the pain you bore for me.

It is said that the following day, her cousin went to the place she had described and found her dead. He carried her inside an enclave and died lying down next to her. The story takes on a legendary turn as it is said that people looking for them found their dead bodies intertwined and buried them locked in their embrace, in a Romeo and Juliet type of ending. Across the mountain an echo was heard reciting the following poem,

The two noble and faithful ones
Are gone in pure loyalty.
By God never I have met,
In all my wandering,
A deeper betrayal or a heavier loss,
Than two dead
On the mountain summit.

33. Suʿdā al-Lakhmiyya

She was from a clan called Lakhm. She was in love with a cousin called ʿĪsā and was apparently not discreet about their meetings and openly said her lover's name. Her family threatened to cut her tongue if she ever mentioned his name again. In response she wrote the following poem,

My body has dried after my long patience,
With words about ʿĪsā that would turn one's hair gray.
I will bear my fondness for ʿĪsā as long as I love him,
Even if for that they cut off my tongue.

34. Sulaimā bint al-Muhalhal

Her father al-Muhalhal had two slaves whom he mistreated. When they were traveling, they killed him. Dying, he implored them to say the following lines to his clan as his will,

Who would tell the people that Muhalhal
May God bless your deeds and those of your father,

When his daughter heard the incomplete lines that did not make sense, she said he was trying to send her a message about his killers. She completed the poem as follows,

Who would tell the people that Muhalhal,
Was killed in the desert by enemies,
May God bless your deeds and those of your father,
Let not the slaves move and kill them.

35. Sumayya Zawjat Shaddād al-ʿAbsī

She was ʿAntara ibn Shaddād's stepmother. She wrote the following poem after his death,

Sleep left me as the night prevailed,
Tears helped me as they flowed.
The loss of a brave man who left and departed,
Is made deeper by my worries.
For who after Shaddād would protect the women
If war broke and sweat glistened?
Who would stop the horses on the day of battle?
And who would stab the enemy in the middle of a siege?
Who would host the guests in his land?
Who would respond to calls for help?
I am in sickness after him,
And my heart because of separation is on fire.

36. Ṭāriqa

She was from the clan of Imru' al-Qais. Her husband was Thābit from the Kalb clan. He married another woman called Nujūd who was rumored to have knowledge of sorcery. When Ṭāriqa heard that, she recited the following lines,

My God grant no good to Abū al-Faṣīl,
And may He never protect him from tripping on easy paths.
He replaced with a vile substitute
Skinny with no flesh, a female ghoul.
With broad hips, she walks slowly like a lazy duck.
May a wolf live in your house and sleep.

37. Tumāḍir bint ash-Sharīd as-Salmiyya

One of the poets of Dāḥis and al-Ghabrā', one of the major tribal wars of pre-Islamic Arabia that started after the end of the Basūs wars. A horse race was organized between two clans of the Ghaṭfān tribe, 'Abs, 'Antara's people, and Dhubyān. The rules of the race stipulated that each tribe chooses one horse. The race would be for a specific distance on a specific track equivalent to one hundred arrows. The loser pays a thousand camels to the winner. Qais, the chieftain of 'Abs chose a horse called Dāḥis and Ḥudhaifa, the chieftain of Dhubyān, chose a mare called al-Ghabrā'. Dāḥis was gaining on al-Ghabrā' but during the race, at a secluded area that could not be seen from either end, a group of men from 'Abs ambushed Dāḥis and lured it off course. Qais heard of the betrayal and in anger killed one of Ḥudhaifa's brothers. In retaliation, Ḥudhaifa killed one of Qais's brothers. This ignited a war that lasted for decades and inspired war poetry, especially by 'Antara, and eulogies, such as this poem. Tumāḍir wrote this poem after her son was killed in one of the battles,

As if the water of my eyes blended with its blood
To a sadness that dissolved its sleep,
Over a boy, the most adorned of all youth.
As if the fire does not see who enkindled it.
If Banū 'Abs mourn him, that is because they have lost their youth.
Who would host the wanderer now,
If the north wind blows, answered by its echo?
Was it your master and protector whom you left
In the desert, its rock now demolished?
Ḥudhaifa, may no stream ever quench your thirst,

And no cloud ever lend you its water,
Just like you tore from me a noble boy,
Who, if weighed against all Banū ʿAbs, would balance the scales.
My tears after him forever will rain,
My eyes shall forever weep.

38. ʿUfaira bint ʿAffān al-Judaisiyya

Her story is sometimes conflated with that of Ukht al-Aswad bin Ghaffār (Ghafīra bint Ghaffār).

39. Ukht al-Aswad bin Ghaffār (Ghafīra bint Ghaffār)

There was a tribe known as Ṭasam and Judais whose king, ʿImlīq, was a tyrant who forced families to offer him their brides on their wedding nights first. Ghafīra the daughter of Ghaffār, the chief of Judais, was getting married and her people willingly sent her to ʿImlīq first. In ʿImlīq's home, while his servants were preparing her for him, they started singing,

Bare yourself and mount with ʿImlīq.
In the morrow strange matters expire.
For you shall get what you did not seek,
And what no one would willingly desire.

To their singing, she replied,

No one more than Judais was so dishonored.
Would their bride be treated thus?
O, my people, what free man among you would accept this
After the dowry and the gifts were paid?
Better to answer death's bidding
Than to have this as a wedding.

After ʿImlīq raped her, she went where her brother al-Aswad bin Ghaffār met his companions to publicly shame him for deserting her. She hiked up her dress to reveal herself in front of them and said,

Does it suit you what to your young men is brought,
While your numbers are like the sand and its grains?
Would you, my people, leave your sister fraught
On the night to a husband she is to be wed?

If this has not to anger led,
Then at home and in bangles a man remains.
With women's perfume you are delighted.
For kuḥl and adornment you were made.
For if we were men and you were women,
We would have not slept if we were slighted.

40. Umaima bint ʿAbdu-l-Muṭṭalib

She was the daughter of ʿAbdu-l-Muṭṭalib, Muḥammad's grandfather. This is Umaima's poem at her father's deathbed,

He passed, he who was the caretaker of the clan,
The provider of water for the pilgrims,
The defender of glory.
At whose house would strangers feel at home,
Now that the skies of everyone else hold back their thunder?
You have been blessed by the best of offspring
Who only add to the gratitude of your graying hair.
The seat of Abū al-Ḥārith that flowed with generosity is now empty,
Do not go far, for all that lives are destined to depart.
May the lord of the people quench your thirst in the grave.
I shall weep for you even in mine.
He was the best of the clan in its entirety,
Worthy of gratitude whenever gratitude would be.

41. Umāma bint Dhī-l-Iṣbaʿ

She was the daughter of the famed poet, Dhī-l-Iṣbaʿ al-ʿUdwānī. She wrote the following poem when she noticed how her father was getting older,

Umāma was struck with fear
When she saw you leaning on a stick,
And remembered the days when we were young.
The arrows of God once struck Irum
And now it's in ʿUdwānī's home.
For after power, virtue, and wisdom,
It is time for time to roam.

Irum was a mythical kingdom, said to have once been of great power and architecture, but nothing remained of its glory. In Qurʾanic stories, it is referred to as Irum of the Pillars and it incurred God's wrath and was completely destroyed.

42. Umāma bint Kulaib at-Taghlibiyya

She is from the powerful Adnanite tribe Taghlib. Since Taghlib was probably a Christian tribe, she could have also been Christian as well. Her tribe is famous for participating in the Basūs war.

The Basūs war between the Bakr and Taghlib clans started when Jassās ibn Murra killed his brother-in-law Kulaib ibn Rabīʿa, Umāma's father. When Kulaib was killed, his wife had a daughter, Umāma who was 12, and was pregnant with a second child. Her brother Jassās took her to their tribe, Bakr, where she gave birth to a son and named him al-Hajras. Jassās raised al-Hajras who married Jassās's daughter. One day, al-Hajras quarreled with a man in the street who told al-Hajras, "Maybe we should do to you what we did to your father." Al-Hajras returned home and asked his mother what the man meant. She told him the truth, that his uncle and father-in-law Jassās had killed his father before al-Hajras was born. Al-Hajras went to Jassās and confronted him. Jassās told him that the war had been over for a long time now and that al-Hajras should find his own peace as well. Al-Hajras agreed but said he wanted to visit his father's people, Taghlib. Jassās agreed and prepared al-Hajras for travel with horses, supplies, and weapons. On the day of his departure, as Jassās was seeing his nephew and son-in-law off, al-Hajras killed Jassās and rode off to his father's clan. Al-Hajras's deed was seen as fair and was justified by his sister Umāma in the following poem,

> You frolic with dice and wine
> And for consequence you never cared.
> You do not know that Kulaib's life
> By Jassās the traitor was not spared.
> Woe to Jassās and ʿAmr
> For the vile deed they dared.

It is possible that Umāma's poem played a role in convincing Jassās's clan, Bakr, to not seek revenge for Jassās.

43. Umm Abī Judāba

She was of Persian descent and her husband of a tribe called the Shaibanīs (not to be confused with the 13th-century Shaibanids who were descendants of Genghis Khan's grandson). Her son, Abū Judāba, fought with his people against Khusrū. His decision to side against her Persian ancestors angered her and she wrote this poem,

> Woe to me for raising such a boy, woe!
> I wished him triumph and victory.

By ill fate he would not properly grow,
He bent to drink disgrace and revelry.
May God curse my milk,
For it was like the milk of a virgin mare
By a mule with a white lock of hair.

44. Umm aḍ-Ḍaḥāk al-Muḥāribiyya

She was from the Muḥārib clan and her husband Zaid, in some accounts ʿAṭiyya, was from the Ḍabāb clan. Their love story is known for its poignant development from marriage to divorce. They remained in love even after their separation. After their divorce, she went to Mecca for a pilgrimage and saw him by the Kaʿba. She went to him and told him the following lines,

Would you leave those you love, when nothing wrong they fare?
You have wronged them, then, and you have been unfair.
Pain keeps me up at night, while you are free of care.
For the life of you, worries seem your sleep to spare.
After Zaid I trust no companion, by God I swear.
Till the stars are no longer there.

In a later poem, she describes her attempts to get over her former husband,

I have overcome my love for Ḍabābī temporarily,
And for those who do not know, my blindness has paid so far.
"You are suspicious," my inner companion told me,
"For the life of me, you are right, for we both are."

The following lines are among the earliest erotic love poems by women in Arabic,

By kissing and embracing love is healed,
When bellies over bellies would grind,
Thrusting till the eyes are sealed,
When necks and heads would bind.

45. Umm al-Aghar bint Rabīʿa at-Taghlibiyya

She was from the tribe of Taghlib. This poem is a eulogy for Ghassān ibn Rawḥān. Ghassān was al-Burāq's brother. Both went to rescue Lailā al-ʿAfīfa when she was abducted by Persians. Ghassān was killed during the attempt.

Weep and do not tire, my eyes.
For in my calamity, I shall always have reason to wail.
Neither is our clan safe, nor has it returned, and to no avail
If noble Ibn Rawḥān dies.

46. Umm aṣ-Ṣarīḥ al-Kindiyya

She and her sister Umm Iyās were from Kinda, born in Ḥaḍramawt, and married from the Banī Kulaib clan. She wrote this eulogy for her sons who died in battle,

The rain watered with their early specks
The corpses of young men in their prime,
And washed the blood off their necks.
They ventured until they were filled with holes
Into the fires of war,
Daring into battle while others
Hid behind the helmets they wore.
Their mother collapsed at the time,
As, on their path to glory,
They were killed in their prime.
With crimson on their necks they would not flee.
They sought no refuge from the fear of death.
If they had fled they would be honored still,
But in welcoming death more honor they could see.

47. Umm Mūsā al-Kilābiyya

Her father Ibn Abī Ḥayyān al-Kilābī married her off to a husband who took her to live in Yemen. She wrote a poem longing for life back in the desert,

Would the door was ajar so I could take a glimpse
Of a land so hard for me to aim for?
If only I could have the desert and its good sands
And a vast land courted by a singing night.

48. Umm Nāshira at-Taghlibiyya

Her son, Nāshira, lost his father at a young age. Hammām ibn Murra took him and raised him as a servant. When Nāshira grew up, however, he found out that his people, the Taghlib tribe, were enemies of Banī Murra. During a battle between both clans, Nāshira had to accompany his master, Hammām. When Hammām was resting from battle, he went for water in his tent, and put his weapon down. Nāshira made use of this, killed Hammām, and escaped to join his clan. His mother expressed her gratitude for Hammām, however, and blamed her son for killing Hammām in her poem,

Nāshira's stab has the lives of orphans misled.
O Nāshira, how ungrateful your right hand can be!
After their chief Kulaib, you have killed the people's head.
No gratitude did you show, but still thankful I would be.

49. Umm Thawāb al-Huzāniyya

There is only one poem by this poet that survived. She wrote a lampoon about her son who disobeyed her,

I raised him like a chick when his feathers were still a fuzz,
Until he left the hive and his stinger started to buzz.
He started beating me and tearing my clothes to tatters.
After my hair is white, do I still need to teach him manners?
I see him comb his beard; the wonder of his facial hair!
Loud enough for me to hear, his wife would tell:
Be gentle, for we still have need of her.
Though if she saw me in the fires of hell,
She would throw in wood, and would not spare.

50. ʿUmra bint al-Khunābis at-Taghlibiyya

Her mother was the daughter of ʿImrān ibn ʿĀmir, king of the Azids. She was married to Lubaid ibn ʿAnbasa al-Ghassānī, who was a Yemeni royal. Yafūr al-Ghassānī, known as the Serpent's Neck, a Ḥimyar title given to the supreme king of kings, chose Lubaid to rule over the Taghlib clan. In order to solidify his position as regent, Lubaid married ʿUmra, a descendant of the local king. Lubaid was hated by the Taghlib clan and they would not pay him taxes. His wife, ʿUmra, sided with her people and argued with him, so he slapped her and said, "You talk as if you were a free woman." She replied, "Why not, am I not a daughter of ʿImrān?" To that he said, "It is because you are a daughter of ʿImrān that I did not tie your hair to the tail of a scabby camel that would run and tear you apart." She left in tears and went to Kulaib one of Taghlib's chieftains, reciting,

I never thought this calamity would befall me,
And I would become a slave for a man from Ghassān,

Until a blow was dealt me by Lubaid,
And I had to cover my face from people's eyes.
Leave not this time humiliated,
Reins should be held until the debt is paid.
If it were not for my lineage,
I would have been torn apart
By a young camel covered in scabs and flammable tar.

Enraged, Kulaib swore to kill Lubaid. He went looking for Lubaid and found him drinking and singing,

Sons of Taghlib, why do you say Kulaib
Sends me the gift of threats?
We were kings at the prime age,
When you were slow slaves.
By denying us the protection money
A war is declared,
And a punishment that makes the newborn's hair gray.
Accept what the king decrees to you,
And do not perish like Thamūd.

Kulaib then went in and killed Lubaid.

51. ʿUtba bint ʿAfīf

She was the mother of Ḥatim aṭ-Ṭāʾī, the legendary figure of hospitality. According to some accounts, she was possibly a descendant of Imruʾ al-Qais ibn ʿAdī ibn Akhzam. She was known for her wealth as well as remarkable hospitality and generosity. Her brothers took control of her money and property to prevent her from giving them away in charity. After forcing her to live in hunger, they eventually gave her some meat from her cattle. Then a woman who used to come to her to receive charity every year visited her as usual. ʿUtba had nothing to give her but the meat, so she gave it to her and recited,

For the life of me, after hunger bit me I swore
To never deny the hungry.
Say this to those who find blame with me:
Forgive me or bite your fingers instead.
What would you tell your sister
But the chastisement of those accustomed to denying?
What you see now is nothing but nature,
So how, sons of my mother, can I my nature abandon?

52. Wahība bint ʿAbdu-l-ʿUzzā

Her family was under the protection of az-Zabarqān ibn Badr ibn Imruʾ al-Qais at-Tamīmī from the Tamīm clan. A man named Huzāl ibn ʿŪf bin Kaʿb from the ʿŪf clan killed her father. She wrote the following poem blaming az-Zabarqān for not avenging her father,

> When would you go to ʿUkāẓ and greet it
> By cutting off noses in public,
> Are you the neighbors of Ibn Miyya, tell me?
> Are you the eyes of Ibn Miyya or are you but useless vows?
> The shame of ʿŪf ibn Kaʿb is stark, so there is no excuse to remove it,
> You and what you hide
> Are like a woman with graying hair who does not have a headcover.

53. Zainab bint Farwa at-Tamīmiyya

She was a member of the Tamīm clan. Her mother was not Arab, possibly Christian Byzantine, and Zainab was clearly proud of that as evident in the following poem describing her mother's beauty,

> Her walk plucks the fruit of youth,
> Shaking what is under her belt,
> Like a soft shooting branch was her youth,
> Shapely like a camel's hump,
> White like uncolored parchment.

54. Zarqāʾ al-Yamāma

She was a pagan priestess, and in some accounts a sorceress. Her name Zarqāʾ refers to her blue eyes. She was from a town called Jaw, and in some accounts al-Yamāma, from the Judais clan in Najd, which belonged to the Yemeni kingdom of Kinda. In classical Arabic folklore, she is said to have had the ability to see people at the distance of three days of walking. She saw an army sent by Ḥassān al-Ḥimyarī, from Ḥimyar, approaching her town and warned her people that soldiers were hiding behind trees that they carried in front of them as they marched towards al-Yamāma. Her people did not heed her warning. As a result, Ḥassān's army swept through the town, destroyed it. Zarqāʾ was captured and blinded. When plucked, it was said that her eyes were filled with kohl. The following is from her poem warning her people of the impending doom,

Be warned, O people, for your own good,
For what I see is not to be scorned.
I see trees and behind them people,
And how do people and trees combine?
Take your people and prepare
For a calamity to be feared and awaited.

The poem ends with the following lines,

Attack those people in their sleep if they lie down,
And fear not their war even if they are many.

Bibliography

ʿAbbūd, Khāzin. *Muʿjam ash-Shuʿarāʾ al-ʿArab min aj-Jāhiliyya ilā Nihāyat al-Qarn al-ʿIshrīn*. Beirut: Rashād Press li-ṭ-Ṭibāʿa wa-n-Nashr wa-t-Tawzīʿ, 2008.

———. *Al-Musīqā wa-l-Ghināʾ ʿInda al-ʿArab*. Beirut: Dār al-Ḥarf al-ʿArabī li-ṭ-Ṭibāʿa wa-n-Nashr wa-t-Tawzīʿ, 2004.

———. *Nisāʾ Shāʿirāt min aj-Jāhiliyya ilā Nihāyat al-Qarn al-ʿIshrīn*. Beirut: Dār al-Āfāq aj-Jadīda, 2000.

Ad-Dusūqī, Muḥammad. *Shāʿirāt ʿArabiyyāt: Ḥallaqna fī Samā ash-Shiʿr Qadīman wa Ḥadīthan*. Cairo: Dār aṭ-Ṭalāʾiʿ, 2009.

Aj-Jāḥiẓ. *Al-Maḥāsin wa-l-Aḍdād*. Beirut: Dār aj-Jīl li-ṭ-Ṭibāʿa wa-n-Nashr wa-t-Tawzīʿ, 1997.

Al-Aṣfahānī, Abū-l-faraj. *Kitāb al-Aghānī*. Edited by Iḥsān ʿAbbās, Ibrāhīm as-Saʿāfīn and Bakr ʿAbbās, Beirut: Dār Ṣādir, 2008.

———. *Al-Imāʾ ash-Shawāʿir*. Edited by Jalīl al-ʿAṭiyya, Beirut: Dār an-Niḍāl, 1984.

Al-Marzabānī, Abū ʿUbaidallah Muḥammad bin ʿUmrān. *Shāʿirāt al-Qabāʾil al-ʿArabīya*. Edited by Sāmī Makkī al-ʿĀnī, Beirut: Ad-Dār al-ʿArabīya li-l-Mawsūʿāt, 2007.

———. *Ashʿār an-Nisāʾ*. Edited by Sāmī Makkī al-ʿĀnī and Hilāl Nājī, Baghdad: Dār ʿĀlam al-Kutub, 1995.

Al-Udhari, Abdullah. *Classical Poetry by Arab Women: A Bilingual Anthology*. UK: Saqi Books, 1999.

Al-Wāʾilī, ʿAbdul-Ḥakīm. *Mawsūʿat Shāʿirāt al-ʿArab: Min aj-Jāhiliyya ḥatā Nihāyat al-Qarn al-ʿIshrūn*, vol. 1/2, Beirut: Dār Usāma, 2001.

Aṣ-Ṣafadī, Ṣalāḥuddīn. *Al-Wāfī bi-l-Wafiyyat*. Edited by Aḥmad al-Arnaʾūt and Turkī Muṣṭafā, vol. 3, Beirut: Dār Iḥyāʾ at-Turāth, 2000.

As-Sayūṭī, Jalāluddīn ʿAbdu-r-Raḥmān ibn Abī Bakr ibn Muḥammad al-Khuḍairī. *Nuzhat aj-Julasāʾ fī Ashʿār an-Nisā*. Edited by ʿAbdu-l-laṭīf ʿAshūr, Cairo: Maktabat al-Qurʾān, 1986.

Aṣ-Ṣūlī, Abū Bakr Muḥammad Yaḥyā. *Ashʿār Awlād al-Khulafāʾ wa-Akhbārahum*. Edited by J. Heyworth-Dunne, vol. 1/2, Cairo: Maṭbaʿat aṣ-Ṣawī, 1936.

Ibn aj-Jawzī, Jamālu-d-dīn Abū-l-Faraj ʿAbdu-r-Raḥmān. *Akhbār an-Nisāʾ*. Edited by Nizār Riḍā, Beirut: Dār Maktabat al-Ḥayā, 1982.

Ibn Ṭaifūr, Abū-l-Faḍl Aḥmad bin Abī Ṭāhir. *Balāghāt an-Nisāʾ wa-Ṭarāʾif Kalāmihunna wa-Milḥ Nawādirihunna wa-Akhbār Dhawāti-r-Rāʾī Minhunna wa-Ashʿārihunna fī aj-Jāhiliyya wa-Ṣadr al-Islām*. Edited by Aḥmad al-Alfī, Cairo: Maṭbaʿat Madrasat ʿAbbās al-Awwal, 1908.

Nujaim, Jūzif. *Shāʿirāt al-ʿArabīya*. Beirut: Dār an-Nahār li-n-Nashr, 2003.

Shirād, Muḥāmmad and Ḥaidar Kāmil. *Mawsūʿat Nisāʾ Shāʿirāt*. Beirut: Dār wa-Maktabat al-Hilāl, 2006.

Wannūs, Ibrāhīm. *Shāʿirāt al-ʿArab*. Beirut: Manshūrāt Miryam, 1992.

Yamūt, Bashīr. *Shāʿirāt al-ʿArab fī aj-Jāhiliyya wa-l-Islām*. Damascus: Ministry of Culture, 2006.

3 Crossover poets

1. ʿAfrāʾ bint ʿUqāl al-ʿUdhriyya

One of the early Islamic tragic love stories. She and ʿUrwa ibn Huzām were in love. One day he died after visiting her and she did not know of his death. A group of people recognized him as her lover. They stopped by ʿAfrāʾ's house and recited,

People of this house, unaware,
We bring you news of the death of ʿUrwa ibn Huzām.

Grief-stricken, she would not believe the messengers and recited back,

Senseless rider, shame on you,
For bringing news of the death of ʿUrwa ibn Huzām.

But the rider confirmed the news by reciting,

Yes, we left him in a faraway rough land,
Staying there where there is no water and no companion.

She finally believed them and recited her request to join them,

If truth you say, then know,
That you have said an obituary
For the moon of every darkness that there is.
For young men after him will find good company,
Nor would they return from their travels in peace,
Nor would a woman give birth to perfect child like him,
Nor would she find joy after him in another boy.

The rest of the story recounts that they took her to his grave. She asked them to leave her alone with him for some time. Soon, however, they heard her scream and went to find her dead next to him. They buried them together.

2. Al-Khansāʾ

Arguably among the most accomplished pre-Islamic and early Islamic poets, al-Khansāʾ's name is Tumāḍir bint ʿAmr ibn al-Ḥārith ibn ash-Sharīd. She became known as al-Khansāʾ, which is a female oryx, and might also mean the snub-nosed one, or the oryx-nosed one. By some accounts, she was the only woman whose poetry was among the great hanging poems.

Al-Khansāʾ started writing before Muḥammad, mainly elegies for the death of her brothers and her sons who were killed in various battles. Her brothers Muʿāwīya and Ṣakhr died before Muḥammad's time in tribal raids. Her four sons, all Muslims, died in the Battle of Qādisiyya between the Muslim and the Sassanid armies.

When she converted to Islam, Muḥammad favored her among the poets and would ask her to recite her poetry for him. It is said that when some complained to him that her eulogies might be interpreted as a rejection of fate, he refused to let them ban her poetry. She outlived Muḥammad, Abū Bakr, and ʿUmar.

In one anecdote, the famous poet an-Nābigha adh-Dhubyānī was in his poetry circle in the ʿUkāẓ market. Next to him were some of the most established poets of the time, such as Ḥassān ibn Thābit. After al-Khansāʾ recited a poem, an-Nābigha told her, "Your poetry is better than that of anyone with a uterus." To which she responded, "By God, my poetry is better than that of anyone with testicles, as well." Ḥassān then challenged them both and all three started a poetry contest. Eventually, an-Nābigha adh-Dhubyānī and Ḥassān ibn Thābit conceded that her poetry was better than theirs.

Her best-known poetry was about the death of her brother Ṣakhr. The following lines are from one of her elegies about him,

> Is there dust in your eyes or are your eyes flawed?
> Or did you weep when the house became of its people free?
> As if my eyes for his memory flowed
> With a flood gushing on my cheeks lavishly.

3. Arwā bint ʿAbdu-l-Muṭṭalib

She was one of Muḥammad's aunts. She converted to Islam and outlived Muḥammad and Abū Bakr. When her father ʿAbdu-l-Muṭṭalib asked his daughters to recite eulogies for him at his deathbed, she recited the following,

My eyes weep as they should weep,
Over a kind face, his nature is humility,
Over man of easy manners, modest,
Generous, whose traits are dignity.
Tall, white, strong, as his forehead is made of light.
He was the one in hospitality and generosity,
And strength when blood is spilt.
When the brave in their armor fear death,
Till their hearts turn to air,
He would advance steadfast steps,
Glory would be surrounding him when you see him.

4. Ash-Shaimāʾ bint al-Ḥarth as-Saʿdiyya

She was from Hawāzin from the Bakr clan. Her birthname might have been Ḥudhāfa. She took the family name of her mother, Ḥalīma as-Saʿdiyya, Muḥammad's wet nurse. She was older than him and was known to recite the following lullaby for him when he was a child,

O God keep our Muḥammad with us,
Till I see him a youth with a moustache.
Then I see him chosen a master.
Suppress his enemies and those who envy him altogether.
And give him dignity that lasts forever.

5. Asmāʾ bint Abī Bakr

The daughter of Abū Bakr, one of Muḥammad's companions and the first caliph. According to some accounts of Muḥammad's life, both men went into hiding to escape from the people of Quraish. They stayed in a cave on the outskirts of Mecca. Asmāʾ used to bring them food and water in pouches tied to two belts around her waist, hence she was nicknamed Dhāt an-Niṭāqain, or The One with Two Belts. She married az-Zubair ibn al-ʿAwwām, one of Muḥammad's companions and they were divorced later. Their son, ʿAbdullah ibn az-Zubair, was killed during the battles between ʿAlī's followers and ʿAbdu-l-Mālik ibn Marwān. Of that she recited,

There is no obedience to God after people
Were killed between Zamzam and the Kaʿba.
Killed by hardhearted goats with fleshy faces and hinds,
And by leper mules.

Her former husband az-Zubair ibn al-ʿAwwām, was killed by ʿAmr ibn Jurmuz while az-Zubair was praying during the Battle of the Camel, one of the early main battles contesting ʿAlī's caliphate, paving the road to the Umayyad caliphate. Asmāʾ and az-Zubair were divorced at the time. She recited the following poem about his death,

> The son of the wolf betrayed a brave knight
> On the day of war and he was not in flight.
> ʿAmr, if you had warned him, you would have seen
> That neither did he miss
> Nor did his heart and hands tremble in fright.
> May your mother mourn you for a Muslim you have slain,
> The curse of the determined murder shall be your plight.

6. Durra al-Hāshimiyya

She is Muḥammad's cousin, the daughter of his uncle, ʿAbdu-l-ʿUzza ibn ʿAbdu-l-Muṭṭalib. As Muḥammad's sworn enemy, he was nicknamed by Muḥammad's early followers as Abū Lahab, or the Father of Fire. She converted to Islam while Muḥammad was still in Mecca before he moved to Medina and followed him there. She recited war poems motivating her clan in the Fijār War, one of the major wars in pre-Islamic Arabia. The Fijār War involved some of the major tribes and was called the War of Sacrilege because the warring factions breached the tradition of not fighting during the four sacred months during which all tribes had agreed to maintain peace for decades. The following are from one of those poems,

> On the morning of war, they met a horse
> Silenced by fear, wearing the armor of Banū Fahr,
> Mute and flawed, whoever sees it
> Thinks it was a wave in the sea.
> The fastest death is the coldest one,
> The most scathing one is the one that takes longer.
> My people, if a rock overpowers them,
> They will be patient
> And the strongest of rocks will scatter.

7. Ḥawma bint al-ʿAjjāj

Her father borrowed from her a calf and kept it for a year and a month. He had a camel called Jawjala, so she asked him to give her the camel instead, reciting the following lines,

Father, may God give you riches and a long life,
And may you live a year and a month,
So you can give me Jawjala with the big mouth.

8. Hind bint ʿUtba

Hind was of high status, the mother of Muʿāwiya ibn Abī Sufyān. It is said that she made a necklace of the ears and noses of those who died among Muḥammad's followers in the Uḥud battle. She is also well known for hiring a slave called Waḥshī to kill Ḥamza, Muḥammad's uncle. When Ḥamza was killed, it was said that she found his body, cut his liver out, and chewed on it, then recited the following lines,

We have paid you back for the day of Badr,
War after war of fire and madness.

It is said that she eventually joined a group of women who went to Muḥammad to convert to Islam in a place called al-Abṭaḥ. Their conversation is often cited. Muḥammad told the group of women to pledge to never fornicate. Her response was to say indignantly, "Would a free woman ever fornicate?" thus pointing out that sex outside of marriage was already taboo in pre-Islamic Arab culture. She outlived Muḥammad and Abū Bakr, had a thriving business in ʿUmar's time. She later supported the Muslim army in the Yarmūk battle against Byzantine armies.

9. Hind bint Uthātha bin ʿAbbād bin al-Muṭṭalib bin ʿAbd Manāf

When Hind bint ʿUtba recited a poem to taunt Muḥammad's followers after she killed Ḥamza, Hind bint Uthātha recited the following lines in response,

Shame on you on the day of Badr and after Badr,
Daughter of the worst of heathens Waqqāʿ.
May God wake you up at dawn tomorrow,
With the Hashemites prospering long,
With every blade that slices,
There remains Ḥamza my lion, and ʿAlī my falcon.

10. Ḥurqa bint an-Nuʿmān bin al-Mundhir

She was the daughter of an-Nuʿmān bin al-Mundhir, the Christian Lakhimid king in al-Ḥīra. Khosrow captured her father, who died in captivity. She joined a monastery near al-Kūfa. During the Islamic conquest, Khālid ibn al-Walīd invited her to convert to Islam. She refused. He ordered a regular pension for her and left her and the monastery unharmed. She recited about this incident praising him,

> He protected my faith and honored my face.
> Only the honorable honors the honorable.

She became a folkloric figure known for anecdotes that display her wisdom. In one anecdote, when Saʿd ibn Abī Waqqās was appointed the ruler of al-Qādisiyya, he requested to see her, having heard of her wisdom as the daughter of a deposed king. She visited him and recited to him a poem about how kingship and all wealth are destined to end, using her lost kingdom as an example,

> While we were leading the people and commands were ours,
> We suddenly became the ones who were led among them
> And in veiling,
> Woe unto a world that allows no bliss to last,
> Turning us upside down again and again.

Saʿd ibn Abī Waqqās rewarded her and blessed her saying, "May God never deprive anyone of His blessings except to make you the cause of restoring those blessings."

In another anecdote, Isḥāq ibn Ṭalḥa ibn ʿUbaid Allah visited her in the monastery seeking her wisdom. He asked her how she managed to withstand the humiliation of losing her father's kingdom. She recited,

> Be patient with what you are fated and be content,
> Even if fate brings you what you do not desire,
> For no one has enjoyed a life that pleases,
> Except to find his joy tarnished by ire.

11. Nutaila

The only thing known about her is that she lost her son during some seasonal festivities. She was known to roam the streets of Mecca reciting,

> I left him in the shade,
> White, intelligent, eloquent, and witty,
> Neither foreign nor adopted,
> On the day of sacrifice in the summer.

12. Ṣafiyya bint ʿAbdu-l-Muṭṭalib

She was one of ʿAbdu-l-Muṭṭalib's daughters. She converted to Islam in Mecca before the hijra to Medina. She is one of ʿAbdu-l-Muṭṭalib's daughters whom he asked to recite elegies for him at his deathbed. She recited the following,

I woke up at night to wailing
Over a man from the high grounds,
So my eyes overflowed on my cheeks
Like water on a sloping mound,
For a generous man with no tightness of hand,
Whose favors are visible on all people,
For the man of flowing charity, and of honor so high,
The father of all good, who inherited all benevolence,
Honest when opinion is called upon, not helpless nor fearful,
Nor harsh was he when he sat nor leaning in weakness,
Tall, of good build, of good status among his clan and obeyed.

13. Ṣafiyya bint Musāfir

A member of the Manāf family, she recited a poem about those killed from Quraish in the Badr battle,

You who have left the eye like a sickness,
Early in the morning and the horns of the sun are still not in flames,
I was told that the lives of noble ones have met their end together for eternity,
That the horse riders ran away,
And that mothers that day had no mercy on their children.
Get up Ṣafiyya and forget not they are relatives.
If you cry, do not cry later.

14. Salmā bint Badr bin Mālik

Her father was killed in the pre-Islamic war of Dāḥis and al-Ghabrāʾ. She converted to Islam and died in Ṭāʾif. She recited about her father's death,

By God's eye, no one has ever seen the like of Mālik
The sad song of his people,
I wish he had never drunk a single drop
Nor went on a single bet.

15. Ukht al-Ḥuṭam

Her brother is al-Ḥuṭam Sharīḥ ibn Ḍabīʿa. He converted to Islam but was among those who would not pay alms to Abū Bakr after Muḥammad died. He was killed during a raid by Salama ibn Qurṭ from the Thaʿlab clan on the Tamīm and Ḍabīʿa clans. His sister recited the following poem about his death,

> They let us wake to a horde of brave and handsome men,
> Led by Ibn Qurṭ like a lion coming out of his den.
> Its knights are of noble lineage from Mālik,
> Among the enslaved noses may be a noble one.
> They killed its renowned knights,
> For a flawed one is not like the flawless one.
> So do not resurrect the war after the truce,
> And let the little ones return with scalped heads.
> And make us weep for the noble ones,
> When we meet tomorrow, with flowing tears.

16. Umm Jamīl bint Umayya

Her name is Arwā bint Ḥarb ibn Umayya but she is known as Umm Jamīl bint Umayya which means the mother of Jamīl and the daughter of Umayya. As the sister of Abū Sufyān ibn Ḥarb and the wife of Abū Lahab, she was among the most powerful women in Quraish. She and her husband were instrumental in persecuting Muḥammad and his followers in Mecca. She is referenced directly in the Qur'ān in the Masad chapter as she is described as wearing a necklace of rope and beads, possibly for sorcery, and is cursed for throwing firewood at Muḥammad. She used to recite the following lines insulting him, referring to him as the Insulted One, which in Arabic would be the opposite of his name, Muḥammad, which, means worthy of praise or the one who is admired,

> The Insulted One we disobey,
> What he brings we reject,
> His religion we hate.

17. Umm Kulthūm bint ʿAbd Wud al-ʿĀmiriyya

She converted to Islam when Muḥammad invited her to join him. Her brother, ʿAmr ibn ʿAbd Wud al-ʿĀmirī, did not convert to Islam and joined a confederate army in a siege against Muḥammad and his followers. In a battle known as al-Khandaq, or the Battle of the Trench, ʿAlī ibn Abī Ṭālib challenged ʿAmr to a duel. ʿAlī killed ʿAmr and Umm Kulthūm recited an elegy expressing how she was torn between her new faith, represented by ʿAlī, and her grief over her brother ʿAmr,

> If ʿAmr was killed by someone else
> I would have wept till the end of time,
> But he was killed by someone who is flawless,
> Someone who was called the unique one.

18. ʿUmra bint Duraid bin aṣ-Ṣamma

She recited a poem about her father who was killed in the Ḥunain Battle, which he lost with Mālik ibn ʿŪf against Muḥammad,

> May God avenge us on Banī Salīm and burden them for what they did.
> May he quench our thirst with the blood of their best when we meet.

Bibliography

ʿAbbūd, Khāzin. *Muʿjam ash-Shuʿarāʾ al-ʿArab min aj-Jāhiliyya ilā Nihāyat al-Qarn al-ʿIshrīn*. Beirut: Rashād Press li-ṭ-Ṭibāʿa wa-n-Nashr wa-t-Tawzīʿ, 2008.

———. *Al-Musīqā wa-l-Ghināʾ ʿInda al-ʿArab*. Beirut: Dār al-Ḥarf al-ʿArabī li-ṭ-Ṭibāʿa wa-n-Nashr wa-t-Tawzīʿ, 2004.

———. *Nisāʾ Shāʿirāt min aj-Jāhiliyya ilā Nihāyat al-Qarn al-ʿIshrīn*. Beirut: Dār al-Āfāq aj-Jadīda, 2000.

ʿAbdu-r-Raḥīm, Muḥammad. *Shāʿirāt Ḥawla ar-Rasūl*. Damascus: Dār Saʿd ad-Dīn, 2011.

Ad-Dusūqī, Muḥammad. *Shāʿirāt ʿArabiyyāt: Ḥallaqna fī Samā ash-Shiʿr Qadīman wa Ḥadīthan*. Cairo: Dār aṭ-Ṭalāʾiʿ, 2009.

Aj-Jāḥiẓ. *Al-Maḥāsin wa-l-Aḍḍāḍ*. Beirut: Dār aj-Jīl li-ṭ-Ṭibāʿa wa-n-Nashr wa-t-Tawzīʿ, 1997.

Al-Aṣfahānī, Abū-l-faraj. *Kitāb al-Aghānī*. Edited by Iḥsān ʿAbbās, Ibrāhīm as-Saʿāfīn and Bakr ʿAbbās, Beirut: Dār Ṣādir, 2008.

———. *Al-Imāʾ ash-Shawāʿir*. Edited by Jalīl al-ʿAṭiyya, Beirut: Dār an-Niḍāl, 1984.

Al-Marzabānī, Abū ʿUbaidallah Muḥammad bin ʿUmrān. *Shāʿirāt al-Qabāʾil al-ʿArabīya*. Edited by Sāmī Makkī al-ʿĀnī, Beirut: Ad-Dār al-ʿArabīya li-l-Mawsūʿāt, 2007.

———. *Ashʿār an-Nisāʾ*. Edited by Sāmī Makkī al-ʿĀnī and Hilāl Nājī, Baghdad: Dār ʿĀlam al-Kutub, 1995.

Al-Udhari, Abdullah. *Classical Poetry by Arab Women: A Bilingual Anthology*. UK: Saqi Books, 1999.

Al-Wāʾilī, ʿAbdul-Ḥakīm. *Mawsūʿat Shāʿirāt al-ʿArab: Min aj-Jāhiliyya ḥatā Nihāyat al-Qarn al-ʿIshrūn*, vol. 1/2, Beirut: Dār Usāma, 2001.

Aṣ-Ṣafadī, Ṣalāḥuddīn. *Al-Wāfī bi-l-Wafīyyat*. Edited by Aḥmad al-Arnaʾūt and Turkī Muṣṭafā, vol. 3, Beirut: Dār Iḥyāʾ at-Turāth, 2000.

As-Sayūṭī, Jalāluddīn ʿAbdu-r-Raḥmān ibn Abī Bakr ibn Muḥammad al-Khuḍairī. *Nuzhat aj-Julasāʾ fī Ashʿār an-Nisā*. Edited by ʿAbdu-l-laṭīf ʿAshūr, Cairo: Maktabat al-Qurʾān, 1986.

Aṣ-Ṣūlī, Abū Bakr Muḥammad Yaḥyā. *Ashʿār Awlād al-Khulafāʾ wa-Akhbārahum*. Edited by J. Heyworth-Dunne, vol. 1/2, Cairo: Maṭbaʿat aṣ-Ṣawī, 1936.

At-Tūnjī, Muḥammad. *Shāʿirāt fī ʿAṣr an-Nubūwwa*. Beirut: Dār al-Maʿrifa, 2002.

Bin Raddās, ʿAbduallah bin Muḥammad. *Shāʿirāt min al-Bādiya*, vol. 1/2, Riyadh: Maṭābiʿ al-Bādiya, 1985.

Bū Falāqa, Saʿīd. *Shiʿr an-Nisā' fī Ṣadr al-Islām wa-l-ʿAṣr al-Umawī*. Beirut: Dār al-Manāhil li-ṭ-Ṭibāʿa wa-n-Nashr wa-t-Tawzīʿ, 2007.

Ibn aj-Jawzī, Jamālu-d-dīn Abū-l-Faraj ʿAbdu-r-Raḥmān. *Akhbār an-Nisāʾ*. Edited by Nizār Riḍā, Beirut: Dār Maktabat al-Ḥayā, 1982.

Ibn Ṭaifūr, Abū-l-Faḍl Aḥmad bin Abī Ṭāhir. *Balāghāt an-Nisāʾ wa-Ṭarāʾif Kalāmihunna wa-Milḥ Nawādirihunna wa-Akhbār Dhawāti-r-Rāʾī Minhunna wa-Ashʿārihunna fī aj-Jāhiliyya wa-Ṣadr al-Islām*. Edited by Aḥmad al-Alfī, Cairo: Maṭbaʿat Madrasat ʿAbbās al-Awwal, 1908.

Nujaim, Jūzif. *Shāʿirāt al-ʿArabīya*. Beirut: Dār an-Nahār li-n-Nashr, 2003.

Shirād, Muḥāmmad and Ḥaidar Kāmil. *Mawsūʿat Nisāʾ Shāʿirāt*. Beirut: Dār wa-Maktabat al-Hilāl, 2006.

Wannūs, Ibrāhīm. *Shāʿirāt al-ʿArab*. Beirut: Manshūrāt Miryam, 1992.

Yamūt, Bashīr. *Shāʿirāt al-ʿArab fī aj-Jāhiliyya wa-l-Islām*. Damascus: Ministry of Culture, 2006.

4 Poets of the early Islamic period

1. ʿĀʾisha bint Abī Bakr

ʿĀʾisha was the daughter of Abū Bakr, one of Muḥammad's closest allies and the first caliph. She was also married to Muḥammad. The following lines were recited by her when her father died,

The water of eyelids is dried out by will,
But concerns and sorrow remain.
Calamities do not end, just because
Their waters were spilled by eyelids and life.

2. Ar-Rabāb bint Imruʾ-l-Qais

She is the daughter of Imruʾ-l-Qais, not the famous poet. She married al-Ḥusain ibn ʿAlī ibn Abī Ṭālib and their daughter Sukaina became a well-known Islamic figure.

She recited the following lines when al-Ḥusain was killed,

He who was the light that brightens for me,
Is now killed in Karbalāʾ uninterred.
Fruit of the Prophet, may God reward you on our behalf,
May you be spared all evil at the scales.
You were for me a high mountain where I seek shelter,
You were a companion for us with faith and mercy.
Who is now the one for orphans and the needy?
Who would shelter the needy and give them till they need no more?
By God I want no family but you,
Until I perish among sand and mud.

3. Asmāʾ Ṣāḥibat Jaʿd

Her name means Asmāʾ the Companion of Jaʿd, referring to Jaʿd al-ʿUdhrī. Their love story is recounted by another established 7th-century poet, ʿAmr ibn Abī Rabīʿa. Abū Rabīʿa was visiting ʿUdhra, and wanted to see its poet Jaʿd, but met Jaʿd's brother who told Abū Rabīʿa that Jaʿd is in a terrible state because of a broken heart, insinuating that Jaʿd, like Abū Rabīʿa is ruined by love and poetry.

Later, when Abū Rabīʿa was in a pilgrimage in Mecca, he saw Jaʿd, who was clearly devastated. Abū Rabīʿa talked to Jaʿd and suggested that Jaʿd pray by the Kaʿba. He overheard Jaʿd mention the day of the oasis in his prayers. When Abū Rabīʿa asked Jaʿd what the day of the oasis was, Jaʿd recounted his story to Abū Rabīʿa.

Jaʿd said that he was visiting his uncles and when leaving they gave him some good wine to take back home. On the road, he stood by an oasis to rest. He saw a horse and a rider approach. The rider dismounted to rest the horse and accompanying mule. They talked for a while, and Jaʿd was so strongly attracted to the rider's wit that he offered the rider a drink. While the rider was drinking, Jaʿd warned him that the flask was hitting the rider's teeth. The rider recited in response,

> If a person kisses another,
> Their teeth he may desire,
> Then he has not sinned and is rewarded.
> If more he seeks,
> Good deeds to his scales shall be loaded,
> By God, until all his sins expire.

As the rider was mounting the horse, Jaʿd noticed the rider's breasts and realized she was a woman. Smitten by the rider's beauty, Jaʿd asked to see her again, but she told him her brothers were fierce and unforgiving and she would not want to see him hurt. She rode on, and left him heart-broken.

Abū Rabīʿa vowed to help his fellow poet and set out searching for the mysterious rider. He finally found her family. He met her brothers who would not let him meet her until he told them he was asking for her hand. Knowing Abū Rabīʿa's status as a famous poet of a good family, they agreed to ask her. He revealed that he wanted her hand in marriage for someone else and urged her brothers to ask her. When they asked her, Asmāʾ recognized the poet she had met in the oasis and approved.

Abū Rabīʿa then describes the fancy wedding Asmāʾ and Jaʿd had. Later, when Jaʿd met Abū Rabīʿa, Jaʿd told him that Asmāʾ explained to Jaʿd why she would not reveal herself as a woman: she wanted to be treated as an equal and to find out Jaʿd's true character, which, like all men, he would not reveal with a woman. She recited the following poem to explain,

When I saw you startled, my love I concealed.
A companion this young man needs, I felt.
If you had known you would have left,
Thinking a girl can be hurt by love or by jest.
What was inside me was not revealed,
But you should know
That, even then, passion inside me reeled.

4. Fāṭima az-Zahrāʾ

Muḥammad's daughter, ʿAlī ibn ʾAbī Ṭālib's wife, and the mother of al-Ḥasan and al-Ḥusain, she is one of the most important cultural Islamic figures. Several anecdotes portray her as the closest of all Muḥammad's children to him. The Fatimid dynasty in Egypt is named after her. She wrote the following lines after Muḥammad's death,

I wish death had found me before it found you,
I would not have mourned you then,
And the book would not have come between us.
Men have frowned at us and have taken us lightly,
Since you left us and all good they have usurped.
Men have showed us the gist of their hearts,
When we lost you, and all inheritance they usurped.

5. Fāṭima bint al-Ḥusain

She was the daughter of al-Ḥusain, Muḥammad's grandson. She wrote the following lines when al-Ḥusain died,

The crow croaked so I told him, "Woe unto you, crow,
Who do you mourn?"
He said, "The imam." The heart of the speaker
Was guided towards the truth.
I said, "al-Ḥusain?" In sorrow, he replied,
"al-Ḥusain is Karbalāʾ, among blades and spears.
I weep for al-Ḥusain with tears,
That satisfy God and earn His rewards."
Then he mounted his wings and could reply no more.

So I wept for what befell me,
After contentment and answered prayers.

6. Ibnat Lubaid bin Rabīʿa al-ʿĀmirī

Her father Lubaid was known for his hospitality. Whenever a desert storm blew on his clan, he would give away some of his cattle to feed those who were in need. One day, al-Walīd ibn ʿUqba, who was a new ruler of Kūfa, was faced with the draught caused by a desert storm. He addressed the people after prayer and asked the people to help Lubaid feed the poor. In order to lead by example, al-Walīd took the initiative by donating one hundred of his cattle to Lubaid's charity and sent them to Lubaid with the following poem,

I see the butcher sharpening his blades,
When the winds of Abū ʿUqail blow,
Noble and proud Lubaid,
With generous arms stretched out
Like a burnished sword.

Lubaid asked his daughter to write a poem as a reply to al-Walīd, as he could not write poetry. She wrote the following lines back to al-Walīd,

When the winds of Abū ʿUqail blew our way,
We then hosted al-Walīd.
Noble-nosed, with glory like the sun's,
Who helped in chivalry Lubaid.
Towering like a hill,
As if the children of Ham were mounting.
Abū Wahb, may God reward you,
We slaughtered the cattle and offered it with bread.

7. Khawla bint al-Azūr al-Kindiyya

She was from Kinda and was known for her bravery, especially during Islamic conquests in the Levant. She died during ʿUthmān's caliphate.

She was among the early women poets to write pride poetry,

We are the daughters of Tubbaʿ and Ḥimyar,
Our strikes among people are undeniable,
For in war, we are fire that scorches,
Today you taste the greatest tortures.

She also wrote elegies for her brother Ḍarār,

Would I enjoy closing my eyes after my brother?
How can a sickly eye know sleep?
I shall weep as long as I live,
For a brother who is dearer than my right eye.

8. Nāʾila bint al-Furāfiṣa

Nāʾila was ʿUthmān ibn ʿAffān's wife when he was the third caliph. Born in Kūfa, her father al-Furāfiṣa was Christian, while she and her brother Ḍabb were Muslims. She wrote to her brother that, although she praised ʿUthmān himself, she was not comfortable living in Medina,

By God, Ḍabb, can't you see, I am accompanied to Medina in caravans,
If they crossed a difficult terrain they hurried,
Shaking like the wind in the holes of canes.
I want the Prince of the Faithful, a brother of piety,
The best of Quraish in status and husbandry.
But among the youth of Ḥiṣn ibn Ḍamḍam,
Those who would not live in houses pulled by ropes.
God has decreed nothing for me
But to become a stranger in Yathrib,
No mother nor father I shall find.

Ḥiṣn ibn Ḍamḍam is Nāʾila's ancestor. Her poem is an interesting contrast to the poem written later by Maisūn bint Baḥdal, Muʿāwiya's wife. While Maisūn preferred life in the desert away from the urban setting of the new Umayyad caliphate, Nāʾila was unhappy leaving the more urbanized Kūfa to go to Medina.

9. Sīrīn ibnat Ḥassān

Her father was Ḥassān ibn Thābit, known as the Prophet's poet, because he wrote several panegyrics praising Muḥammad. She frequently entered into poetry contests with and against her father. Once, it is said that Ḥassān could not sleep so he recited,

How come if the consequences of matters overwhelm us,
We take the branches and uproot the roots?

He then stopped. She asked him whether he could not finish the lines and he said he could not and challenged her to finish them for him. She recited,

> Good sayings that in dignity speak no debauchery,
> Give a clan what it asks for.

Her lines inspired Ḥassān and he recited,

> A rhyme like spearheads befell me,
> I received its descent from the distant skies.

To which she recited,

> Seen by Him in whose presence no poetry is uttered,
> And whose words no one can emulate.

Ḥassān was so impressed by his daughter's poetry that he told her, "I shall say no more verse as long as you live," which while usually an exaggeration, is said as the highest of compliments from one poet to another. To his compliment, she replied, "And to this I add, that neither shall I."

10. Umm-ul-Aswad al-Kilābiyya

She was from the Kalb clan. She was well known for her lampoons about her husband.

> I shall warn every white woman,
> Soft and well-mannered, of noble lineage,
> Of a man of short stature, closer to his slippers,
> He spends his morning tired,
> And in the evening
> Sleeps by the fire after dinner.
> If he says he is full, then he is content,
> And hides in his wide white nightdress.
> He considers it a shame for perfume to touch his clothes,
> Or musk if one day its scent on him is found.

11. ʿĀʾisha bint ʿAbdu-l-Mudān

Her name is ʿĀʾisha bint ʿAbdu-l-Mudān. Her husband was ʿUbaidullah ibn ʿAbbās who was appointed by the caliph ʿAlī ibn Abī Ṭālib as governor for Yemen. During the war between Muʿāwiya and ʿAlī, Muʿāwiya sent Sirr ibn Arṭṭā to Yemen to impose Mu'āwiya's rule over lands controlled by 'Alī and his followers there. It is said that 'Abbās escaped when he heard that ibn Arṭṭā's army was approaching, leaving his wife and their two sons. Sirr killed both sons. It was said that 'Ā'isha bint 'Abdu-l-Mudān would roam the streets reciting the following lines about them,

You who took away the brothers,
Know that it is their mother who is bereaved,
Wondering if someone saw her sons,
Asking for water, but not given any.

12. Umm Ḥakīm bint Yaḥyā

She was known for spending a fortune on wine. She wrote some of the earliest wine poetry in the early Islamic period,

Quench my thirst with your rosy drink
If I have spent all my money, pawn my cloak,
My bracelet, and my bangles.
Everything I own is rightfully yours to loot,
So do not cut off my roses.

13. Umm Ḥamāda al-Hamadhāniyya

She was known for her love poetry. Below are two poems she wrote,

Love went around all God's worshippers,
Until it reached me and stopped.
I wonder at a heart infatuated by you,
But in return gets neither gentleness nor gratitude.

I complained to her the pain of love,
She said, you lied to me, I still see your flesh on you.
Wait, then, till love and longing inflict your bones,
Until they shiver in the open valleys.
Until the whispers of love possess you,
And you are completely mute to those who call your name.

14. Umm 'Uqba Zawjat Ghassān bin Jahḍam

Her story is told as part of tales recounted to entertain prince Khālid ibn 'Abdullah al-Qasrī, Umayyad ruler of Mecca. The story refers to an earlier time. Umm 'Uqba's husband Ghassān bin Jahḍam once asked her what she would do after his death. She promised to never marry if he died and recited reassuringly,

> I shall keep Ghassān, in spite of his far abode,
> I shall care for him, until we meet for the final day.
> I am from all people distracted, so enough,
> It is not I who would betray.
> I shall weep for him as long as I live, with tears
> That roam my cheeks only to multiply.

The story goes on, however, narrating that after her husband died, she did after all marry another man. One night her husband visits her in her dreams and reminds her of her poem. She was so distraught by his visit that she took her own life when she woke up.

15. ʿUmra bint Ruwāḥa

Her brother was ʿAbdullah ibn Ruwāḥa, one of Muḥammad's companions. Two of her sons, Lu'ai and Ghālib, died in the battle of Badr. She recited the following lines for them,

> My eyes cry among those who cry for Badr and its people,
> And flows with tears for Lu'ai and Ghālib.
> Let them know for certain and let them see,
> Their armies sweep over beards and moustaches.

16. Zainab bint al-ʿAwwām

She was the sister of az-Zubair ibn al-ʿAwwām, one of Muḥammad's early followers. Her father, al-ʿAwwām ibn Khuwailid, was the brother of Khadīja bint Khuwailid, Muḥammad's first wife. Her son ʿAbdullah ibn Ḥakīm, was killed during the Camel Battle between ʿAlī ibn Abī Ṭālib's followers and Muʿāwiya's. She wrote about her son's death,

> My eyes be generous with your tears and fast,
> For a generous man with open hands,
> We pray for Zubair and ʿAbdullah,
> Close to our heart and our only pregnancy.
> You have killed the Prophet's disciples, family, and friends,
> Bear now the omen of hellfire.
> I was broken before when Bin ʿAffān was killed,
> My sighs profusely gave him my tears.

I am certain now that faith is in retreat,
For how can we after him pray and fast?
How can we and how can the faith be,
After Ibn Arwā and Ibn Umm Ḥakīm?
You have denied ʿUthmān's water in his home,
May you drink like cattle from boiling water.

17. Zainab bint ʿUqail bin Abī Ṭālib

Her father is mentioned as ʿAlī ibn Abī Ṭālib's brother, and one of Muḥammad's followers. She recited the following lines when ʿAlī and Fāṭima's son, and Muḥammad's grandson, al-Ḥusain was killed in Karbalāʾ.

What would you say to the Prophet if he asked you
What have you done as the last people
With my family and my brethren after my departure?
Some of them prisoners of war, and others lie in their blood.
Is this what I receive in return for my advice to you,
You succeed me by hurting my kin?

Bibliography

ʿAbbūd, Khāzin. *Muʿjam ash-Shuʿarāʾ al-ʿArab min aj-Jāhiliyya ilā Nihāyat al-Qarn al-ʿIshrīn.* Beirut: Rashād Press li-ṭ-Ṭibāʿa wa-n-Nashr wa-t-Tawzīʿ, 2008.

———. *Al-Musīqā wa-l-Ghināʾ ʿInda al-ʿArab.* Beirut: Dār al-Ḥarf al-ʿArabī li-ṭ-Ṭibāʿa wa-n-Nashr wa-t-Tawzīʿ, 2004.

———. *Nisāʾ Shāʿirāt min aj-Jāhiliyya ilā Nihāyat al-Qarn al-ʿIshrīn.* Beirut: Dār al-Āfāq aj-Jadīda, 2000.

ʿAbdu-r-Raḥīm, Muḥammad. *Shāʿirāt Ḥawla ar-Rasūl.* Damascus: Dār Saʿd ad-Dīn, 2011.

Abū ʿAlī, Nabīl Khālid. *Shāʿirāt ʿAṣr al-Islām al-Awwal: Dirāsa Naqdiyya.* Cairo: Dār al- Ḥaram li-t-Turāth, 2001.

Ad-Dusūqī, Muḥammad. *Shāʿirāt ʿArabiyyāt: Ḥallaqna fī Samā ash-Shiʿr Qadīman wa Ḥadīthan.* Cairo: Dār aṭ-Ṭalāʾiʿ, 2009.

Aj-Jāḥiẓ. *Al-Maḥāsin wa-l-Aḍḍād.* Beirut: Dār aj-Jīl li-ṭ-Ṭibāʿa wa-n-Nashr wa-t-Tawzīʿ, 1997.

Al-Aṣfahānī, Abū-l-faraj. *Kitāb al-Aghānī.* Edited by Iḥsān ʿAbbās, Ibrāhīm as-Saʿāfīn and Bakr ʿAbbās, Beirut: Dār Ṣādir, 2008.

———. *Al-Imāʾ ash-Shawāʿir.* Edited by Jalīl al-ʿAṭiyya, Beirut: Dār an-Niḍāl, 1984.

Al-Marzabānī, Abū ʿUbaidallah Muḥammad bin ʿUmrān. *Shāʿirāt al-Qabāʾil al-ʿArabīya.* Edited by Sāmī Makkī al-ʿĀnī, Beirut: Ad-Dār al-ʿArabīya li-l-Mawsūʿāt, 2007.

———. *Ashʿār an-Nisāʾ.* Edited by Sāmī Makkī al-ʿĀnī and Hilāl Nājī, Baghdad: Dār ʿĀlam al-Kutub, 1995.

Al-Udhari, Abdullah. *Classical Poetry by Arab Women: A Bilingual Anthology*. UK: Saqi Books, 1999.

Al-Wā'ilī, 'Abdul-Ḥakīm. *Mawsū'at Shā'irāt al-'Arab: Min aj-Jāhiliyya ḥatā Nihāyat al-Qarn al-'Ishrūn*, vol. 1/2, Beirut: Dār Usāma, 2001.

Aṣ-Ṣafadī, Ṣalāḥuddīn. *Al-Wāfī bi-l-Wafiyyat*. Edited by Aḥmad al-Arna'ūt and Turkī Muṣṭafā, Beirut: Dār Iḥyā' at-Turāth, 2000.

As-Sayūṭī, Jalāluddīn 'Abdu-r-Raḥmān ibn Abī Bakr ibn Muḥammad al-Khuḍairī. *Nuzhat aj-Julasā' fī Ash'ār an-Nisā*. Edited by 'Abdu-l-laṭīf 'Ashūr, Cairo: Maktabat al-Qur'ān, 1986.

Aṣ-Ṣūlī, Abū Bakr Muḥammad Yaḥyā. *Ash'ār Awlād al-Khulafā' wa-Akhbārahum*. Edited by J. Heyworth-Dunne, vol. 1/2, Cairo: Maṭba'at aṣ-Ṣawī, 1936.

At-Tūnjī, Muḥammad. *Shā'irāt fī 'Aṣr an-Nubūwwa*. Beirut: Dār al-Ma'rifa, 2002.

Bin Raddās, 'Abduallah bin Muḥammad. *Shā'irāt min al-Bādiya*, vol. 1/2, Riyadh: Maṭābi' al-Bādiya, 1985.

Bū Falāqa, Sa'īd. *Shi'r an-Nisā' fī Ṣadr al-Islām wa-l-'Aṣr al-Umawī*. Beirut: Dār al-Manāhil li-ṭ-Ṭibā'a wa-n-Nashr wa-t-Tawzī', 2007.

Ibn aj-Jawzī, Jamālu-d-dīn Abū-l-Faraj 'Abdu-r-Raḥmān. *Akhbār an-Nisā'*. Edited by Nizār Riḍā, Beirut: Dār Maktabat al-Ḥayā, 1982.

Ibn Ṭaifūr, Abū-l-Faḍl Aḥmad bin Abī Ṭāhir. *Balāghāt an-Nisā' wa-Ṭarā'if Kalāmihunna wa-Milḥ Nawādirihunna wa-Akhbār Dhawāti-r-Rā'ī Minhunna wa-Ash'ārihunna fī aj-Jāhiliyya wa-Ṣadr al-Islām*. Edited by Aḥmad al-Alfī, Cairo: Maṭba'at Madrasat 'Abbās al-Awwal, 1908.

Nujaim, Jūzif. *Shā'irāt al-'Arabīya*. Beirut: Dār an-Nahār li-n-Nashr, 2003.

Shirād, Muḥāmmad and Ḥaidar Kāmil. *Mawsū'at Nisā' Shā'irāt*. Beirut: Dār wa-Maktabat al-Hilāl, 2006.

Wannūs, Ibrāhīm. *Shā'irāt al-'Arab*. Beirut: Manshūrāt Miryam, 1992.

Yamūt, Bashīr. *Shā'irāt al-'Arab fī aj-Jāhiliyya wa-l-Islām*. Damascus: Ministry of Culture, 2006.

5 Analysis

Poetics of rejection

The poetry of Umayyad and Abbasid women offers interesting stylistic and thematic diversity, as the poems in the second part of this anthology highlight a movement away from traditional elegies and religious poetry of pre-Islamic and early Islamic poetry. Nevertheless, studies in English of Umayyad and Abbasid poetry still remain to a noticeable extent informed by poetry written by male poets of the same periods as seen for instance in Schoeler's "The Genres of Classical Arabic Poetry Classifications of Poetic Themes and Poems by Pre-Modern Critics and Redactors of Dīwāns." Women poets of the periods from the 7th to the 15th centuries CE are largely read within the trajectories of male poets. Schoeler classifies Arabic poetry according to genres and traditions (5). While genres such as campsite poetry, as well as panegyrics and invectives, for instance, are recognizable features of Arabic poetry, they have consistently been used in reference to poetry written by men and, therefore, using them as standards for reading poetry by women can be limiting to understanding the full wealth of a substantial part of classical and Medieval Arabic poetry.

On the other hand, attempts to highlight specific themes and genres in reading women's poetry can expand the horizon of the study of women poets. It can expand studies about the true scope of women's Medieval Arabic poetry, as the narrowing down of genres for women poets lends itself to an essentialist perspective of Arabic poetry of women, rendering it as primarily poetry of elegies, for instance.

Alternative readings of poems by women during that period can shed light on poetry written by women for women. It is possible to see women as acting. One such reading can be in the light of the women needing to recreate themselves in order to fit within the new narrative during the period referred to as Umayyad to Abbasid poetry, perhaps as part of the expectations of women to "recast their identities" to fit with the new evolving context of Islamic culture, as El Cheikh puts it (115). Women were noticeably more empowered in the creative world of literature than their counterparts of other contemporary cultures. The number of women poets, more than 200 in this anthology, more than half of whom produced poetry before the 10th century, surpasses the number of women poets anthologized for Hellenistic and Latin poetry during the same period. While, for instance, Sappho is traditionally mentioned as the only woman among the best-known Hellenistic poets, Barnard argues that there are more poets not frequently mentioned, but she limits those to nine poets only (204). As for Latin poetry, Stevenson writes that, with the exception of four poets, Sulpicia, Proba, Hrotsvitha, and Heldigard, "guides to Latin literature, however apparently comprehensive, seldom mention women" (1). Poetry for Arab women during the Umayyad and Abbasid ages was a source of social acceptance and mobility, as their poetry was appreciated all the way up to the court (Segol 147). It is interesting to read the poetry of this relatively large number of Arab women poets as attempts to forge a place oscillating between response and initiation.

There are clear instances where women take initiatives in major genres such as *ghazal*. We see that when Ḥafṣa bint al-Ḥāj ar-Rukūniyya takes the initiative of calling on a lover, possibly Aḥmad ibn ʿAbd an-Nabī, she writes,

> Do I visit you or do you visit me,
> For my heart leans to what yours desire.
> (Al-Wāʾilī 1: 128)

Explicit *ghazal* was also common in Umayyad and Abbasid poetry by women. This is evident, for instance, in the poem by Khadīja bint al-Maʾmūn,

> By God tell that buck with the heavy buttocks
> And a waist so small,
> He is sweetest when he is ready,
> And, when in ecstasy,
> He is the most gorgeous of all.
> (Al-Wāʾilī 1: 156)

Bint al-Maʾmūn feminizes the eroticization of gazelles, traditionally a male poetic metaphor when describing women as sexualized objects of desire. In her poem, the male lover she describes is given the animal symbol of a buck, thus using the same male context but switching its content by changing the gender of the sexualized object.

These instances, however, do not constitute a common occurrence where women wrote poetry that is not found in the genres dominated by male poets. This chapter proposes that, perhaps, it is the poetry of rejection that offers a poetics where women poets prevailed. Poetry of rejection gave women poets access to other subgenres of poetry, such as *ghazal*, invectives, and lampooning, as well as Bacchic poetry.

It is possible to argue for the significance of looking into a form of empowerment in poetry that women wrote at the time by identifying a poetics that characterized that poetry. This empowerment is exemplified by rejection found in the poems discussed in this chapter that shed light on how the female poets responded to situations they did not initiate. Examples of these range from marriage proposals to moving to an urban setting after marriage, with other examples of a negative response such as commentary on the consummation of marriage and even a poet's depiction of the scene where she and her lover met that contradicts the lover's description. It is possible, in that sense, to view those poems as a means of empowerment, reinforcing an element of choice women planted in their poems when reacting to situations imposed or created by men. For the most part, those poems can be viewed as creative outlets through which women poets created a poetics of rejection.

The categories of rejection in the poems are linked to choice. Whether the poems express a choice the poet made or a contradiction and defiance of a choice a male figure made earlier, the poems reinstate a level of agency to the poets in their reclaiming of choice by making it or by challenging it. The rejection in the poems can be categorized thematically. There are four contexts in which the poems of rejection and choice seem to figure prominently. One is a spatial context. Poems that fall within this category are related to place as a contested domain of male hegemony. Another is the body. Most of the Classical poems written by Arab women dealing with the body manifest an affirmation of ownership. The third context is wine. Bacchic poetry, *khamriyyat*, is a major genre of classical Arabic poetry, and in the poetry written by women wine is positioned at an interesting intersection between the feminine and masculine principles. The fourth context is the rejection of mainstream narratives which posit masculinity at their center.

Reclaiming space

An Umayyad example of a rejection poem with a spatial context is Maisūn bint Baḥdal's nostalgic poem. Married to the founder of the Umayyad caliphate, Caliph Muʿāwiya, she moved to the caliph's palace from her home as the daughter of Baḥdal ibn Unaif, the chief of Banī Kalb, a large Syrian Orthodox Christian Bedouin tribe of Palmyra that constituted a critical mass for Umayyad presence in Syria. Her movement with Muʿāwiya after their marriage in 645 can be seen as a stereotypical move that women in many cultures have made to accompany their husbands (Freeland 89). In her case, specifically, the movement is supposed to constitute significant progress on the socio-political scale. Maisūn, however, takes an interesting approach towards her transition. She views it within the context of urbanization, a substitution of lifestyles, and her poem, sometimes referred to in some earlier translations as the "Song of Meysūn," offers an unflattering comparison between her origins in a rural Bedouin setting and her new life in urban settings of the rising Umayyad caliphate (Redhouse 268). Her poem goes,

> A house throbbing with people
> Is more pleasing to me than a lavish palace.
>
> A dog that barks to drive wanderers away from me
> Is more pleasing to me than a tame cat.
>
> Wearing a cloak and being content
> Is more pleasing to me than wearing sheer clothes.
>
> Eating a small crumb in a corner in my home
> Is more pleasing to me than eating a loaf.
>
> The sound of the wind in every path
> Is more pleasing to me to than the strumming tambourines.
>
> A difficult calf that follows howdahs,
> Is more pleasing to me than a fast mule.
>
> Among my cousins a weak and slender-built one
> Is more pleasing to me than an overfed ass.
>
> My rough life among the Bedouins
> Is sweeter to me than soft living.
>
> For all I want is my homeland instead
> Suffice it to say for me that it is a land of honor.
>
> (Al-Wāʾilī 1: 578–9)

Maisūn's comparison underlines the binaries, the dualities inherent in many poems of Arab women that address rejection and choice. The barking dog of the rural life as opposed to the domesticated cat of the urban palace, crumbs of bread and a whole loaf, rough cloak preferred to fancy fabric, howling winds better than royal cymbals and drums. It is possible to notice here the rustic elements of idyllic life, glorifying the wild (wild barking, wind) over the artificial (domesticated, drums). Yet, it is also significant to notice the glaring economic aspects of comparing the standards of life before and after marriage to the caliph and movement to urban life: rough and rich fabric, crumbs and loaf, house and palace. Perhaps the most outstanding of all the pairs is the last one, preferring a poor, skinny man of her kindred to the overfed mule of urban life. It is hard not to make the assumption that the overfed mule might be a reference to Muʿāwiya. Indeed, Freeland recounts how Muʿāwiya was not flattered at knowing his wife describes him as an overfed mule and would prefer a skinny man of her tribe to him and, as a result sent her and her son Yazīd back to her family (89).

Whereas Maisūn's rejection of the space chosen by Muʿāwiya leads to a rejection of Muʿāwiya's lifestyle, Andalusian poet Ḥafṣa bint al-Ḥāj ar-Rukūniyya challenges a male notion of place but does not reject the person himself. Ḥafṣa had a relationship with Abū Jaʿfar ibn Aḥmad that ended in his fall from favor with the governor of Granada, Abū Saʿīd ʿUthmān, who was all the more powerful as the son of ʿAbdul-Mūʾmin. ʿUthmān competed with Abū Jaʿfar for Ḥafṣa's attention and Abū Jaʿfar was eventually executed for the family feud between Abū Jaʿfar's Banī Saʿīd and ʿAbdul-Mūʾmin's. Ḥafṣa and Abū Jaʿfar apparently met in a grove and Abū Jaʿfar wrote a poem that depicted an idyllic picture of the grove that protected and blessed the secret meeting of the lovers,

God ever guard the memory
Of that fair night, from censure free,
Which hid two lovers, you and me,
Deep in Muʾammal's poplar-grove;
And, as the happy hours we spent,
There gently wafted a sweet scent
From flowering Nejd, all redolent
With the rare fragrance of the clove.
High in the trees a turtle-dove
Sang rapturously of our love,
And boughs of basil swayed above
A gently murmuring rivulet;
The meadow quivered with delight
Beholding such a joyous sight,
The interclasp of bodies white,
And breasts that touched, and lips that met.
(Arberry 94; I am citing Arberry's
translation for both poems)

Abū Jaʿfar's fervently pleasant view of the grove is wholly rejected by Ḥafṣa, who writes,

Do not suppose it pleased the dell
That we should there together dwell
In happy union; truth to tell,
It showed us naught but petty spite.
The river did not clap, I fear,
For pleasure that we were so near,
The dove raised not his song of cheer
Save for his personal delight.
Think not such noble thoughts as you
Are worthy of; for if you do
You'll very quickly find, and rue,
High thinking is not always wise.
I scarce suppose that yonder sky
Displayed its wealth of stars on high
For any reason, but to spy
On our romance with jealous eyes.
(Arberry 95)

The much darker, even sinister, description of the same place offered by Ḥafṣa sharply contradicts with Abū Ja'far. Indeed, given what we know of the tragic end Abū Ja'far met, it is possible to claim his outlook was not as grounded in reality as Ḥafṣa's was. Her rejection runs deeper than challenging Abū Ja'far's take on the scene where they had their sexual escapade. Her rejection signals a more mature outlook and a more perceptive understanding of the socio-political atmosphere the lovers lived in and that eventually did have a tragic end that is much closer to Ḥafṣa's interpretation than Abū Ja'far's "noble thoughts."

Reclaiming the body

Another context for the poetry of rejection is related to the body. The female body in some poems acts as a testimony to the failed male attempts at hegemony and control. Umayyad poet Shaqrā' bint al-Ḥubāb's poem referred to a man called 'Amr in her poem. While there is no consensus as to who 'Amr is, he is most likely her husband as understood from her poem. 'Amr whips Bint al-Ḥubāb because of her love of Yaḥyā ibn Ḥamza. Her poem uses her body as testimony of her abuser's weakness,

I tell 'Amr as the whip circles around my body,
Lashes are the most wicked proof it's true.
So bear witness, you who is jealous, that I love him.
Flog me, but the one who is humiliated is you.
(Al-'Aqqād 113)

The circular movement of the whip envelops both the abuser and the abused. They are both interlocked around the female body. The defiant response from Bint al-Ḥubāb denies the physical pain and turns it back to the inflictor of pain, ʿAmr, who is humiliated not only by her love for Yaḥyā, but by whipping her, as that act of violence only proves his jealousy and externalizes it even further, causing him humiliation. The female body is, therefore, central to the male humiliation twice, both with the failure to own it and with the display of humiliation when trying to punish it.

A common situation that combines the female body with failed male dominance was seen in poems about the impotence of a male partner, an incident that resulted in a number of lampoons and invective poems. Umm al-Ward al-ʿAjlāniyya writes,

> If you want to know how that night prevailed,
> The old man teased me again and again,
> Until the time before dawn, and then
> When he put the key in the lock, it failed.
> And when he thundered, there was no rain.
> (Shirād 94)

Ridiculing impotence is also seen in a poem by ad-Dahnāʾ bint Misḥāl. Aj-Jāḥiẓ recounts her story (232). When her marriage to Umayyad poet, al-ʿAjjāj, was not consummated, she and her father officially complained and requested her divorce. When al-ʿAjjāj was confronted by her request, he embraced her. In response, she recited,

> Move away from me. You cannot have me
> With kissing, embracing, or scent.
> (Aj-Jāḥiẓ 232)

The description of male impotence as a failure is linked to public humiliation in both poems. A legal complaint against al-ʿAjjāj is central to ad-Dahnāʾ's poem. The implication of gossip is stated in al-ʿAjlāniyya's first line, "if you want to know what happened." This type of rejection is evident primarily in responses to marriage proposals or propositions of a relationship.

In addition to impotence, marriage proposal is a major theme that poets used to reclaim agency of their bodies. ʿAʾisha al-Qurtubiyya, in her response to a marriage proposal, compares herself to a lioness who has rejected lions before and would, therefore, never accept a dog. Gazelles are traditionally metaphors of women's femininity in Arabic literature (Hartman 39). The distinctive metaphor of a woman as a lioness in this Andalusian poem stands in interesting contrast to the more common metaphor of women as gazelles.

In ʿA'isha's poem, the metaphorical rejection sets the female speaker apart as an individualized gendered person,

> I am a lioness but, for the life of me,
> To become someone's mount
> I shall never allow myself.
> And if so I ever choose to be,
> A cur I would not count,
> When to lions my ears were deaf.
> (Al-Wāʾilī 2: 382)

Perhaps the elements of choice and agency of the body are best represented by Andalusian poet, Wallāda bint al-Mustakfī, who was known for sewing two lines of poetry on her clothes (Shirād 354). On the right side she sewed,

> By God I am fit for the highest of peaks
> And I walk my walk and boast in pride.

While on the left she sewed,

> I enable my lover to have my cheeks.
> And if someone craves a kiss, I provide.
> (Al-Wāʾilī 2: 676)

The focus on consent is evident in linking choice, represented by choosing who gets a kiss, to honor, represented by the high peaks. This links consent and agency to pride and the individuality of "walk my walk." It is even more telling knowing that Wallāda's highlighting of consent is paired with her decision not to wear any sort of veil (Segol 159).

Reclaiming the mind

Bacchic poetry was a long-standing genre in Classical Arabic literature, with poets such as Abū Nūwās excelling at weaving wine into serious arguments of defiance and choice, being "a master of all genres" of Arabic poetry (Colville 3). Arab poetry about wine by women seems, however, to challenge the celebratory tone in Bacchic poets such as the tone Abū Nūwās adopts. Their poems link wine to loss of mental faculty. A case in point is the poet, Ṭaqiyya bint Ghaith aṣ-Ṣūriyya,

> There is nothing good in wine,
> Though mentioned as a feature of Paradise.

For if it blends with the sane,
Madness would bring his demise.
He'd fear a downfall so steep,
Leaving the heart with no guise.
(At-Tilmisānī 2: 603)

The poet reinforces her point by playing with three words that change meaning only by changing the diacritics; hence, *janna* means Paradise, *jinna* means madness, and *junna* means guise. The wordplay boasts a sharp mind while mocking slurred pronunciation with the change of diacritics.

Umm al-ʿAlāʾ al-Ḥijāriyya al-Barbariyya laments being unable to use wine for its effect on the mind. She focuses on how wine does not sit well with love and poetry,

If only wine did not disagree
With longing and singing so,
Among wine cups you'd find me,
Making all my wishes grow.
(Al-Maghribī 114)

It is interesting how al-Barbariyya sees poetry and love as requiring of some measure of control and concentration that would be numbed by wine. In addition, her choice not to drink wine does not stem from religious edicts, but from her conviction that wine would ruin her sense of control of her emotions and her talents. Instead of challenging the common stereotypical link between all three, she acknowledges its existence and admits she desired to drink it, then clearly challenges it.

Reclaiming the narrative

Male-structured themes and motifs in poetry are interwoven in a narrative constructed by male perspectives as well. Among the areas of rejection in women's poetry during that period was challenging the narratives set by men. Perhaps nothing can be more deconstructive in that respect than challenging the narrative of one's own lover. The Qais and Lailā love story is built around Lailā and *majnūn*, or Lailā and her madman, thus centering Qais at the heart of the narrative as the victimized lover. Lailā challenges this narrative by arguing that Qais at least had the luxury of publicly declaring his love, while she had to suffer like he did, but only in silence,

The Madman suffered nothing
That I as well had not felt,

But he told the secret of love,
While I, in silence, would melt.
(Al-Wā'ilī 1: 523)

Lailā's challenge of the suffering of the male lover weighs in with the social restrictions of silence that are imposed specifically on women in cases of a forbidden love gone public.

This theme of silence is recurrent in women's poetry, particularly in relation to publicly speaking of a relationship or even saying a lover's name. ʿUlayya bint al-Mahdī was Hārūn ar-Rashīd's sister (Al-Heitty 185). Awareness of her brother's status clearly made it even harder for her not to keep her love life secret. Her poetry, however, expressed rejection of that notion,

The heart for Rayb is yearnful,
O Lord, how is that shameful?
(Aṣ- Ṣūlī 1: 20)

ʿUlayya's poem was directed at a servant she had (Al-Heitty 192). It is possible that this is an example of homoerotic poetry between her and a woman named Zainab. In another account, the name Zainab was a nickname that ʿUlayya gave to a man named Ṭull (Al-Heitty 192). According to that account, when ʿUlayya sensed that her brother's court might find out the identity of her lover, she changed the nickname to Rayb. She explained that she chose that name playing with the letters *r*, *y*, and *b* and the diacritic *a*, which is short for the long vowel ā, because those letters can form the two words, *Rayb* and it can be reordered to form the phrase yā rab, which means, O Lord (Aṣ- Ṣūlī 1: 20).

The motif of silence is tackled by Āsiya al-Baghdādiyya as well. She was given as a gift to ʿAbdullah ibn Ṭahir, a high-ranking officer of al-Maʾmūn. She remained silent for days (Al-Wā'ilī 1: 22) until he rebuked her for her silence and asked her if she was "dumb." To that she said,

Silence, of two alternatives, is the one with favored consequence for me,
And, for me, it is better than an utterance of dispute.
(Aṣ-Ṣafadī 258)

Āsiya's response turns quickly into defiance as she says,

Do I brandish a weapon among those who do not know it?
Or do I sprinkle pearls among the blind in the dark?
(Aṣ-Ṣafadī 258)

With those two lines, al-Baghdādiyya situates herself above those abusing her silence. She explains that her silence is more out of mercy for them as her words are a weapon they do not know, referring to her superiority as a poet. She goes even further and describes her words as pearls and, returning the insult of describing her as dumb, she describes the listeners as blind who would not see her pearls. She even hints at the entire atmosphere being dark, thus referring to Ibn Ṭahir's company as a whole being unenlightened. Her silence, then, is because the men in her company would neither value nor keep up with what she is capable of saying.

As an antithesis to silence, Medieval Arab women, particularly during the Abbasid age, engaged in the practice of poetry contests that were commonly associated with male poets in pre-Islamic times up to even the early Umayyad age (Al-Heitty 48). This changed gradually and it became a common occurrence for women to compete with men in poetry. One example is the poet ʿInān, who, according to one account, was bought and raised by someone referred to as ʿAbdu-l-Malik an-Nāṭāfī (Al-Heitty 114). He allowed her, and possibly used her, to compete in poetic contests professionally when she displayed poetic talents. She contributed to turning his house into a *majlis* (assembly), or literary salon (Al-Heitty 114). The group of poets known as *al-Mājinūn* (the depraved), that included none other than Abū Nūwās himself, met at her *majlis*. There are stories of the poets competing with the aim that the winner will hold the salon at her or his house. After each poet recited a poem, they all agreed that ʿInān's poem was the best and the salon remained in her house (Al-Heitty 260–62). ʿInān's poetic status enabled her to excel in poetic contests against the likes of Abū Nūwās, who, in fact, engaged in competitions with her more than any other poet (Al-Heitty 120).

That same *majlis* witnessed another exchange that adds to the challenging of male-dominated narratives. The poet ʿAbdullah al-Qāsim ibnʿIsā challenged another poet, Faḍl, by saying,

> They said you loved a young one, I told them
> The most delicious ride is one not mounted before.
> Such a difference there is between a pierced pearl,
> And that which was never pierced afore.
>
> (Al-Heitty 120)

Faḍl replied using the same meter and rhyme scheme,

> A ride is not a joy to mount
> Unless tamed and mounted before,

And pearls are of no use to their owners,
Unless they have been pierced and threaded afore.
(Al-Heitty 235–6)

The two poems are interesting in their open conversation about virginity, arguably an established form of male hegemony over women as it is central to how sexual activity has been used to judge women on more than one level. Faḍl's poem strongly challenges the notion of preference of virginity when she argues that women who are sexually active make better lovers. What Faḍl's poem contributes here is using a traditionally male-centered context for her poem: male pleasure. Ibn ʿIsā's erotic lampoon, probably directed at Faḍl herself, holds virginity at high esteem, not from a conventionally conservative perspective that associates virginity with morality but from a male-centered perspective that defends Ibn ʿIsā's own choices of a much younger lover making the choice rest on whatever brings more pleasure to men. Faḍl uses that same context and challenges it by arguing that such pleasure is attained only with women who have prior sexual experience.

Interestingly, poetics of rejection at first reading may be seen as rising from a response to poems and narratives set forward by the patriarchal structure of the literary mainstream. Nevertheless, those reactionary poems grew into a tradition of their own that not only defined Medieval Arab women's poetry, but also set them apart as poems of defiance and writings of assertive identity.

Ḥafṣa bint al-Ḥāj ar-Rukūniyya once sent a note to Abū Jaʿfar,

A visitor has come with a gazelle neck
Yearning to the crescent under the wings of darkness.
(Al-Wāʾilī 1: 128)

Ḥafṣa here reclaims the gazelle. As a common metaphor from animal symbolism used in classical Arabic literature to describe women, it traditionally referred to features such as docility, innocence, and flightiness, thus, by contrast, highlighting the male lover's strength, experience, and courage. Not in this poem. Ḥafṣa is rewriting that metaphor as the gazelle is not passively watched by a lover from a distant, ready to take flight before she is hunted. She is the visitor boldly visiting her lover and even asking in the same poem,

What do you say of letting the gazelle in,
Or maybe it is interrupting some business?
(Al-Wāʾilī 1: 130)

ʿĀʾisha al-Qurtubiyya's lioness rejects lions and dogs alike and chooses to live life according to her choices. Ḥafṣa does not do away with gazelles. Instead, she rewrites what a gazelle can mean. It is interesting, and perhaps rather symbolic, that Ḥafṣa is an Andalusian poet and her age, perhaps, signals the last phase of what is frequently referred to as the Golden Age of Arabic and Islamic culture. Perhaps what made that age so distinguished was the ability to rewrite the heritage of the gazelle and pair it with the metaphor of the lioness, and claim them both.

Bibliography

Aj-Jāḥiẓ. *Al-Maḥāsin wa-l-Aḍḍād*. Beirut: Dār aj-Jīl li-ṭ-Ṭibāʿa wa-n-Nashr wa-t-Tawzīʿ, 1997.

Al-ʿAqqād, ʿAbbās Maḥmūd. *ʿArāʾis wa-Shayāṭīn*. Cairo: Muʾassasat Hindāwī, 2012.

Al-Heitty, Abdul-Kareem. *The Role of the Poetess at the ʿAbbāsid Court (132–247/750–861): A Critical Study of the Contribution to Literature of Free Women and Slave-Girls under the Early Abbasid Caliphate: Their Biographies and Surviving Works*. Beirut: Al Rayan, 2005.

Al-Maghribī, Abū al-Ḥasan ʿAlī ibn Saʿīd. *Al-Maghrib fī ḥulī al-Maghrib*. Edited by Shawqī Ḍaif, Cairo: Dār al-Maʿārif, 1955.

Al-Wāʾilī, ʿAbdul-Ḥakīm. *Mawsūʿat Shāʿirāt al-ʿArab: Min aj-Jāhiliyya ḥatā Nihāyat al-Qarn al-ʿIshrūn*, vol. 1/2, Beirut: Dār Usāma, 2001.

Arberry, Arthur John, translator. *Moorish Poetry: A Translation of 'The Pennants,' an Anthology Compiled in 1243 by the Andalusian Ibn Saʿīd*. Cambridge: Cambridge UP, 1953.

Aṣ-Ṣafadī, Ṣalāḥuddīn. *Al-Wāfī bi-l-Wafiyyat*. Edited by Aḥmad al-Arnaʾūt and Turkī Muṣṭafā, vol. 3, Beirut: Dār Iḥyāʾ at-Turāth, 2000.

Aṣ-Ṣūlī, Abū Bakr Muḥammad Yaḥyā. *Ashʿār Awlād al-Khulafāʾ wa-Akhbārahum*. Edited by J. Heyworth-Dunne, vol. 1/2, Cairo: Maṭbaʿat aṣ-Ṣawī, 1936.

At-Tilmisānī, Aḥmad bin Muḥammad al-Maqrī. *Nafḥu aṭ-Ṭīb min Ghuṣn al-Andalus ar-Raṭīb*. Edited by Iḥsān ʿAbbās, vol. 1/2, Beirut: Dār Ṣādir, 1968.

Barnard, Sylvia. "Hellenistic Women Poets." *The Classical Journal*, vol. 73, no. 3, 1978, pp. 204–13.

Colville, Jim. *Poems of Wine and Revelry: The Khamriyyat of Abu Nuwas*. Abingdon, UK: Routledge, 2014.

El Cheikh, Nadia Maria. *Women, Islam and Abbasid Identity*. Cambridge, MA: Harvard UP, 2015.

Freeland, Humphrey William. "Gleanings from the Arabic: The Lament of Maisun, the Bedouin Wife of Muâwiya." *The Journal of the Royal Asiatic Society of Great Britain and Ireland*, new series, vol. 18, no. 1, Jan., 1886, pp. 89–91.

Hartman, Michelle. "Gender, Genre, and the (Missing) Gazelle: Arab Women Writers and the Politics of Translation." *Feminist Studies*, vol. 38, no. 1, spring, 2012, pp. 17–49.

Redhouse, James W. "Observations on the Various Texts and Translations of the So-Called 'Song of Meysūn': An Inquiry into Meysūn's Claim to Its Authorship;

and an Appendix on Arabic Transliteration and Pronunciation." New Series of *The Journal of the Royal Asiatic Society of Great Britain and Ireland*, vol. 18, no. 2, Apr., 1886, pp. 268–322.

Schoeler, Gregor. "The Genres of Classical Arabic Poetry Classifications of Poetic Themes and Poems by Pre-Modern Critics and Redactors of Dīwāns." *Quaderni di Studi Arabi*, vol. 5/6, 2010, pp. 1–48.

Segol, Marla. "Representing the Body in Poems by Medieval Muslim Women." *Medieval Feminist Forum: A Journal of Gender and Sexuality*, vol. 45, no. 1, 2009, pp. 147–69.

Shirād, Muḥāmmad and Ḥaidar Kāmil. *Mawsū'at Nisā' Shā'irāt*. Beirut: Dār wa-Maktabat al-Hilāl, 2006.

Stevenson, Jane. *Women Latin Poets: Language, Gender, and Authority from Antiquity to the Eighteenth Century*. Oxford: Oxford UP, 2008.

6 Umayyad poets

1. Ad-Diḥdāḥa al-Faqīmiyya

She was from the al-Faqīm clan. When the famous lampoonist al-Farazdaq wrote a poem about her clan, she responded with the following poem,

A soft drooping glans,
With a head too close and incomplete.
A louse with soft stubble,
Tight with a stinger sliding out,
I inserted that in
Al-Farazdaq's anus.

It is said that al-Farazdaq feared her lampoons so much, he avoided her when he saw her. She would not let him get away without another lampoon, however,

If the dove flew away, in its nest he'd sleep,
Here is my place, so in yours you stay.
Like al-Farazdaq, of defective birth like sheep,
Who, when he saw me, in defeat ran away.

2. Al-ʿAjliyya

Her name is unknown. She was from the ʿAjlī clan and survived a plague in Baṣra during the rule of Musʿab ibn ʿUmair. She lost most of her family to the plague. When she heard a wolf at night, she recited,

O wolf calling before daybreak,
Shall I tell you what appeared to be?

I saw that I have become a mother,
That I am the one left of a family
Who bequeathed but tears to me.
There is no harm, then, if I follow those who left,
And be followed by those who shall be next.

3. Al-Ḥusainiyya

Her name is not known. She is only mentioned in an account by Ibn ash-Shaiẓamī. He said he overheard a woman at the Ka'ba praying and saying how poor she was. When he approached her and offered to help her, she rejected him and recited indignantly,

Some of the daughters of men have been
Pushed out by time and left out to see,
Pushed out of the glory of bliss,
Became needy and deprived.
She was the one whose caravan
When she went out attracted many eyes.
If He has saddened and hurt her now,
He has for so long pleased her and given her joy.
Gratitude be to the God of hard times,
For He has guaranteed to lift her hardship.

He said he inquired about her and found out she was related to al-Ḥusain.

4. Al-Kinãniyya

She is known for confronting 'Abdullah ibn Yaḥyā al-Kindī, from Kinda in Yemen, when he roamed around trying to gain public support to become a caliph and depose Marwān ibn Muḥammad. When she saw al-Kindī she told him,

Would you rule us from Ḥaḍramawt?
You ask for kingship from afar.
Was it Kinda, man, or Quraish
In Mecca that knew the laws and codes?

5. Ḥafṣa bint al-Mughīra

She married Ḥanṭab ibn 'Abdullah al-Makhzūmī and clearly hated him. She lampooned him on more than one occasion as in the following lines,

Why would I not weep and cut my hair,
When white virgins marry Ḥanṭab?

In the following poem, she warns all women against marrying unattractive men of a lower social status,

Trust not life after me,
For the free white women marry Ḥanṭab.
A sly son of the black-bottomed she-wolf,
Stingy, with her family milking her dry breasts.
I was thrown around lineages till I landed
Among a long lineage of men of short stature.

6. Ḥumaida bint an-Nuʿmān ibn Bashīr al-Anṣārī al-Khazrajī

Her father was the governor of Ḥimṣ. She married three times, and in some accounts four. She wrote lampoons about all her husbands.

About her first husband, Ibn ʿAbdullah ibn Khālid, who was an immigrant to Ḥimṣ, she wrote,

The old and young of Damascus are dearer to me,
Than the newcomers.
Their odor is like that of goats,
Overwhelms musk and amber.

Her brother arranged her marriage to her second husband, Rawḥ ibn Zinbāʿ. She wrote a poem blaming her brother for marrying her off to Rawḥ,

May God misguide you, boy,
When did we marry lepers?
Do you accept the legs and tails of cattle,
Though we used to be offered the humps of camels?

Her third husband, al-Faiḍ ibn Abī ʿUqail al-Thaqafī, was a drunk. She lampooned him in the following poem,

I am an Arab mare,
The offspring of steeds mounted by a mule.
If I produce a noble colt then it is from my side,
But if it is a mixed breed, then that is
What is fathered by this bull.

7. Jāriyat Sulaimān ibn ʿAbdu-l-Malik

In an anecdote about the caliph al-Maʾmūn, when Abū ʿĪsā died, al-Maʾmūn was distraught. He asked Abū al-ʿAtāhiya to tell him a story about someone in a similar condition. The well-known Abbasid poet Abū al-ʿAtāhiya recounted that once Sulaimān ibn ʿAbdu-l-Malik wore his best clothes and best perfume, and asked his servant to describe him. She recited,

> You are the most blissful of joys, if only you were to stay,
> But there is no staying for any man.
> You are devoid of flaws and what may cause dismay,
> Yet you are also just a mortal man.

Abū al-ʿAtāhiya added that Sulaimān looked away, frowning. He died the same week. When al-Maʾmūn heard this anecdote, he wept.

8. Lailā al-Akhyaliyya

Her father was ʿAbdullah ibn ar-Raḥḥāl. He was nicknamed al-Akhyal, from the Arabic word *al-khail* which means horses, and al-Akhyal means the best horseman, as he was a distinguished knight. She was one of the most accomplished Arab poets. In addition to her poetry, she became such a legendary cultural icon, that there are several anecdotes about her that highlight how empowered and independent she was, shedding light on the rapidly changing status of women in the Umayyad community.

She was close to al-Ḥajjāj who knew of her escapades but would not hurt her. According to one anecdote, she was already married when she fell in love with a man called Tawba ibn al-Ḥimyar. Her love for Tawba was an open secret that everyone knew about including her husband, and was at times tolerated and at others frowned upon. She would normally cover her face when she went to meet him. When she heard that al-Ḥajjāj was sending guards to arrest Tawba, she went to their meeting without covering her face, so he understood that she was being watched and left before the guards arrived.

She defied even al-Ḥajjāj himself. He once hinted that he desired her, and she shamed him by reminding him that they were both married to others by reciting the following poem,

> To him who has a need we said, disclose not your need
> For never in your life, there shall be a way to what you seek.
> We have a companion we should not betray,
> And you rightfully belong to another one and to her you are committed.

When she aged, the Umayyad caliph ʿAbdu-l-Malik ibn Marwān told her in jest, "What does Tawba see in you now that you have aged so?" She retorted, "What people saw in you when they made you caliph." He laughed at her wit.

When Tawba died, Lailā's health deteriorated quickly. She was traveling with her husband in a caravan. When they passed by the graveyards where she knew Tawba was buried, she insisted on dismounting and visiting his grave against her husband's disapproval. When she went, she addressed the grave greeting Tawba, then turned to her companions and told them, "This is the first time Tawba lies to me." When they asked her how would he have lied, she told them that he had promised to always greet her back even if he were dead, and recited the following poem,

> If Lailā came to greet me,
> and I am under soil and crusts of land,
> She would greet me with a smile,
> Or an echo would hoot to her by my grave,
> And then I would have from Lailā what I could not have,
> For whatever the eyes are content with is good.

The tales about her death would have it that after this incident, while she was going back to her caravan, an owl flew by, scaring the camel, which in turn threw Lailā off and she fell, hit her head, and died. She was buried next to Tawba.

9. Lailā bint Mahdī (also Lailā al-ʿĀmiriyya)

She and Qais ibn al-Mulawwaḥ are the iconic star-crossed lovers of Arab literary heritage. The story of Lailā and Majnūn (madman) is a story of family feuds and denied love that has set the tone for tragic love stories in countless literary, musical, and cinematic adaptations until the present time. Among many illustrations and paintings that depict the lovers, Persian miniatures by Ferdowsi provide a visual narrative of their story.

There are numerous accounts of their love. Lailā and Qais ibn al-Mulawwaḥ were from the same clan and grew up together. They are often depicted as two youths from wealthy families, who would meet at first among their entourage of companions and servants, until they started meeting alone. Their love, however, was highly publicized from the beginning. When they fell in love, Qais wrote prolifically about Lailā, including describing her body intimately. Such attention drew outraged reactions from both families as they considered public love scandalous. Both families attempted to separate the lovers. Lailā's family forced her to marry a man called Ward al-ʿUqailī. It is said that Qais roamed the deserts alone, giving away all his possessions, until he was driven insane, hence the nickname Laila's Madman. In some accounts, some people took pity on the lovers and united them, but it was too late as Qais was already dying and Lailā, grief-stricken, died shortly after.

While Qais has gained most of the fame as poet in cultural reproductions of the tale, Lailā, an established poet in her own right, was often overshadowed by Qais's poetry, even during their lifetime. She wrote the following poem about how her suffering was sidelined because she was silenced while at least he expressed his pain,

The madman was not in a state,
That I myself have not felt.
But he revealed the secret of love,
While in silence I would melt.

In another poem, when their families decided to stop them from seeing each other, she urged Qais to be patient,

I would sacrifice myself for you,
If only myself I owned.
For none but you deserve it
And bring it content.
Patience, then, for what God has decreed
Upon you in me.
There is bitterness in my patience
That I hide within me.

Once, he saw her talking to another man, and was heart-broken. She recited to him the following poem, explaining to him that she had to pretend that she was no longer in love with him to protect him from her family who had threatened to kill him,

Hatred in front of people we both display,
But each one of us is in the other's deepest parts.
What we want our eyes to us would say,
As love is buried in the depths of our hearts.

10. Lailā bint Yazīd bin aṣ-Ṣaʿq

She is known mainly because of her husband, Ziyād ibn Abī Sufyān, who was one of the four Shrewd Arabs (*duhāt al-ʿArab*), the others being ʿAmr ibn al-ʿĀṣ, Muʿāwiya ibn Abī Sufyān, and al-Mughīra ibn Shuʿba. Her husband Ziyād was an interesting figure in the transitional period from the

Rashidun caliphate to the Umayyad. Of uncertain lineage, he was given the humiliating nickname Ziyād ibn Abīh (Zīyād the Son of His Father). It was often speculated that he was the bastard son of Abū Sufyān. As the chief tax collector of *bait al-māl* (House of Money), he remained loyal to ʿAlī ibn Abī Ṭālib, however, and would not join Muʿāwiya against ʿAlī. He was promoted governor of Istakhar, one of the Sassanid provinces controlled by ʿAlī. Nevertheless, when ʿAlī was killed and Muʿāwiya took over, he offered a peace treaty with Ziyād on the condition that Muʿāwiya would acknowledge Ziyād's lineage and would finally claim him as his brother and allow him to formally use the name Ziyād ibn Abī Sufyān. Ziyād agreed and became the governor of Kūfa and an ardent protector of Muʿāwiya's rule.

Lailā wrote the following poem after their son died,

> You were a mountain I took shelter in its shade,
> Then you left me walking in a valley open and dry.
> You were my protection as long as you lived,
> I walked in the open and you were my wings.
> Today I avoid the undignified and to Him I succumb,
> I put my hand up to protect myself from those unjust to me.

11. Maisūn bint Baḥdal

Her father Baḥdal ibn Unaif was the chief of the Kalb clan in Palmyra and eastern Syrian deserts, and her family joined the Syriac Orthodox church. She was married to Zāmil ibn ʿAbdu-l-Aʿlā whose brother was killed during the conflict that led to Muʿāwiya's caliphate. Her family avoided taking sides in the conflict between Muʿāwiya and ʿAlī, and, as a result, Muʿāwiya married her to strengthen his presence in the Levant deserts.

When she moved with Muʿāwiya to the urbanized parts of the Levant, she did not like life in royal courts and wrote what has become one of the most widely read and translated poems by a classical Arab woman,

> A house throbbing with people
> Is more pleasing to me than a lavish palace.
>
> A dog that barks to drive wanderers away from me
> Is more pleasing to me than a tame cat.
>
> Wearing a cloak and being content
> Is more pleasing to me than wearing sheer clothes.
>
> Eating a small crumb in a corner in my home
> Is more pleasing to me than eating a loaf.

The sound of the wind in every path
Is more pleasing to me to than the strumming tambourines.

A difficult calf that follows howdahs (caravans),
Is more pleasing to me than a fast mule.

Among my cousins a weak and slender-built one
Is more pleasing to me than an overfed ass.

My rough life among the Bedouins
Is sweeter to me than soft living.

For all I want is my homeland instead
Suffice it to say for me that it is a land of honor

It is said that after writing this poem, she and Muʿāwiya were divorced and she returned to live with her family. However, as the mother of Muʿāwiya's son, Yazīd, who succeeded his father as caliph, she remained an influential figure in early Umayyad politics.

In some accounts, her poem is attributed to another poet called Maisūn bint Jandal. Yet, it is also possible that bint Baḥdal was, indeed, the one who wrote that poem but perhaps Orientalist translators glossed over the fact that a Christian poet married a Muslim caliph, and later Umayyad enthusiasts also tried to deny such an embarrassing episode happened to the powerful Umayyad caliph.

12. Rābiʿa al-ʿAdawiyya

One of the most celebrated Islamic mystics as well as literary figures, her life is usually narrated as an example of wisdom and spirituality. The most recurrent story of her life is that she was a slave from Baṣra whose master, from the ʿAtīk family, freed due to her piety. While there are different accounts of her life, the one constant element in all of them is the motif of penitence and a spiritual oneness with the supreme being, usually depicting such union in sensual terms. Her poetry is a major influence on Sufi poetry and Arabic poetry in general. She is still a cultural icon in contemporary Muslim communities, with television shows and films depicting her at times as a freed slave and at others as a repenting sex worker.

In one of her best-known poems, she defines the notion of divine love which has become a major feature of Sufi poetry later on,

I love you two loves,
A love of love,
And a love because that is what you deserve.

As for the love of love,
It keeps me away from anyone but you.
As for that which you deserve,
It is that you removed all veils
Till I saw you.
There is no gratitude due to me
For either this or that.
But all gratitude goes to you
For this and for that.

In another poem, she highlights the distinction of flesh and soul,

I put you in my heart to speak to me
And left my body to whomever sits with me.
Thus, they can have the company of my body,
While the love of my heart
Would keep my heart company.

13. Saʿda bint Farīd bin Khaithuma bin Nūfal bin Naḍla (also Umm al-Kamīt)

She, her husband Aʿsha ibn Asad, and her son, al-Kamīt, were all poets. Her son married Bint Abī Mahwūsh against Saʿda's will, so she recited the following poem to reproach him,

Go for the debris of noble lineage,
And take a friend among the noble women.
For the life of me, Sa'da's son has plucked himself short,
With short feathers of the tail,
Instead of feathers of the front wings that are long.
A lineage was built for you but you wrecked,
Honor has those who build it and those who pull it down.

14. Shaqrāʾ bint al-Ḥubāb

She was married to a man named ʿAmr and fell in love with a man named Yaḥyā ibn Ḥamza. Her poetry is among the few surviving poems about the theme of extra-marital relationships in Umayyad poetry,

Yaḥyā's love has wiped that of my husband.
For Yaḥyā the beginning and end of our love.
I'd give up my father for Yaḥyā, and the fold of his clothes,
And his waist where his sword is holstered.

She is best known for her powerful poem about domestic abuse as she recites a poem describing how the fact that her husband hit her proved only his humiliation rather than hers,

> I tell ʿAmr as the whip circles around my body,
> Lashes are the most wicked proof it's true.
> So bear witness, you who is jealous, that I love him.
> Flog me, but the one who is humiliated is you.

15. Umaima Imraʾat ibn ad-Damīna

She was married to Ibn ad-Damīna, whose real name was ʿAbdullah ibn 'Ubaid-Allah and who went by his mother's name, from the Salūl clan. It is said he used to write love poetry for his wife while courting her but when she agreed to marry him, he mistreated her. She wrote a poem reproaching him,

> You are the one who abandoned your promise,
> And caused those who blamed me to gloat.
> You displayed me in front of the people then left me,
> An object to be targeted by them while you remain unharmed.
> If words left marks on our bodies,
> My body would be scarred by the words of those who bear no secrets.

It is said he apologized to her upon hearing this poem. Later, however, it was said that he found out she was having an affair with a man from his clan, Salūl. He killed both his wife and her lover. In retaliation, the Salūl clan sent someone to kill him.

16. Umm al-Barāʾ bint Ṣafwān (Barra bint Ṣafwān)

She was an ardent supporter of ʿAlī and was famous for her fearless poems against Muʿāwiya. An anecdote about her is recounted as an example of the aftermath of the war between ʿAlī and Muʿāwiya. It was said that after ʿAlī died, she went to Muʿāwiya. When he saw how she was old and poor, he reminded her of a poem she wrote to motivate ʿAlī's men against him,

> In haste and readiness saddle your steed
> For war, never rise for flight.
> The call of the imam you heed,
> March under his flag with might,
> Pounce on the enemy with the sharpest blade.

I wish my body was not in shame perceived,
I would have defended him
From the soldiers of the depraved.

He then asked her what she needed, but she indignantly refused and left. He sent her money and clothes, saying, "If I lose patience, then who would keep it?"

17. Umm al-Ward al-ʿAjlāniyya

She was from the ʿAjlān clan. She was known for her erotic poetry. In one occasion, she was alone with a younger lover and she told him,

Are you obeying me, my tiger cub, once,
Then in betrayal disobeying me when the sun breaks,
Making it a world with only a shade to live in,
Its well is dry and its lands are without pasture?

She wrote one of the earlier poems of *ghazal ṣarīḥ* or explicit courtly poetry by a woman in classical Islamic literature,

Might there be a young man in whose organ
The water of youth is kept in its vigor?
Walking with a strong claw close to his knee,
Curved, but not due to flawed creation?

18. Umm Sinān bint Khaithama bin Khursha al-Madhḥajiyya

She once went to the Umayyad caliph Muʿāwiya to complain that Marwān ibn al-Ḥakam, the governor of Medina, imprisoned her grandson unjustly. In an anecdote rather similar to what happened with Umm al-Barāʾ, it is said that Muʿāwiya recognized her as one of ʿAlī's supporters in the past, and one of his aides reminded him of her poem against Muʿāwiya,

You perished father of Ḥusain but still
You are guided by truth and so you do guide.
Go may peace be on you as long as
A singing dove rests on a branch.
You were after Muḥammad for us his successor,
He asked you to care for us
And to his words you were loyal.

Today no other successor after him we hope for,
Never would we praise after him another human.

She did not deny writing the poem, and told Muʿāwiya that it was people around him, like the man who reminded him of the poem, that had once made him unpopular and that Muʿāwiya should rule with justice and mercy like his people, the Manāf clan, would rule. Muʿāwiya admired her eloquence and sent orders to Ibn al-Ḥakam to free her grandson.

19. Umm Walad li-Hishām bin ʿAbdu-l-Malik

She had a child with Hishām ibn ʿAbdu-l-Malik, but there is no record of her name or whether they were married. She recited the following poem in praise of her son from him,

If they mix our water with theirs,
They come to you like rubies in their features,
They would admire them for their deeds,
And would refer the fellow to his father.

20. ʿUmra bint al-Ḥamāris

She was known for her humorous obscenities. It was said that her father did not want her to get married. Once, she saw him sharpening fence pickets, and approached him while reciting the following poem,

Who would tell a single man about the unmarried
Daughter of al-Ḥamāris, the short old man with thick haunches,
The girl whose legs are shapely and knees are round,
And who would rock and shake when a phallus is found?

21. ʿUmra bint Mirdās

She was al-Khansāʾ's daughter. Like her mother she wrote mainly elegies. Her two brothers, Yazīd and al-ʿAbbās died. The following poem was for al-ʿAbbās,

My eyes have not betrayed you,
The time and days have refused to grant my eyes patience.
I feared not to seem
Like a beast weeping its kin in loss.
You see the rival gloating in fake pride,
While he was far from a match to my brother.

22. ʿUṣaima bint Zaid an-Nahdiyya

She married a man from her clan named Saʿīd ibn Salīm and called Abū as-Samaidaʿ, which means the father of generosity. She hated him and lampooned him in the following poem,

They say ʿUṣaima did not receive her dowry.
Cursed be those who blame ʿUṣaima.
If they had been through what I experienced,
They would follow me and would seek no dowry.
Saʿīd ibn Salīm's odor is like
The odor of land wet by the urine of foxes.
If I flee him, I would be locked up all night,
God forbid anything else is desired.

23. Zawjat Abī al-Aswad ad-Duʾalī

Her husband Abū al-Aswad al-Du'alī was one of Muʿāwiya ibn Abū Sufyān's generals and trusted aides. Ad-Du'alī divorced her and wanted custody of their son. She went to Muʿāwiya while ad-Duʾalī was sitting next to him and asked for his judgment. When ad-Duʾalī and his wife exchanged accusations, Muʿāwiya remarked that she was much more eloquent than her husband. He asked each one of them to make a claim for the child. Ad-Duʾalī said, "I bore him before she bore him and delivered him before she delivered him." His wife then said, "He bore him lightly and I bore him heavily. He delivered him in pleasure and I delivered him in pain."

When ad-Du'alī noticed how impressed Muʿāwiya was with her, he recited a poem chastising her,

Greetings to her who unfairly accuses us,
Welcome to the carrier and the carried.
She closed her door to me and said,
The best of women is the one with a husband.
She kept herself too busy for me with nothing to do,
Have you ever heard of one who is free and busy?

She replied with a poem of her own,

He who uttered in righteousness and in foolishness,
Is not like he who unfairly went astray from the well-lit path,
My breast fed him in the morning,
My lap was his courtyard by sunset.

I want nothing, Ibn Ḥarb,
Except this weak little one you know.

Apparently inspired by the poetic turn of the trial, Muʿāwiya then delivered his verdict in a poem as well,

She who fed him when he was an infant,
And gave him her breasts, is not to be let down.
She is more deserving of him, and closer kin
Than his father, by virtue of revelation and scripture.
For her love and care of him,
She is more deserving of this tiny one.

24. Zawjat Hishām bin Ṭulba bin Qais

She went to the judge Ibrāhīm ibn Hishām al-Makhzūmī and asked for divorce claiming her husband was impotent. When he denied that, she recited the following poem publicly,

Hishām is a liar and was not truthful,
Hishām slipped at the slippery place.
His breaking wind left no love,
Like a mare turning away,
Repulsed by a tiring mule.
Ibn Hishām, you tall one,
Of undisputed lineage,
The sly one lied and was not truthful.

Bibliography

ʿAbbūd, Khāzin. *Jamīlāt al-ʿArab kamā khalladahunna ash-Shuʿarāʾ*. Beirut: Dār al-Ḥarf al-ʿArabī li-ṭ-Ṭibāʿa wa-n-Nashr wa-t-Tawzīʿ, 2013.
———. *Muʿjam ash-Shuʿarāʾ al-ʿArab min aj-Jāhiliyya ilā Nihāyat al-Qarn al-ʿIshrīn*. Beirut: Rashād Press li-ṭ-Ṭibāʿa wa-n-Nashr wa-t-Tawzīʿ, 2008.
———. *Al-Musīqā wa-l-Ghināʾ ʿInda al-ʿArab*. Beirut: Dār al-Ḥarf al-ʿArabī li-ṭ-Ṭibāʿa wa-n-Nashr wa-t-Tawzīʿ, 2004.
———. *Shuʿarāʾ Qatalathum Ashʿaruhum wa-Ḥubbuhum*. Beirut: Dār al-Āfāq aj-Jadīda, 2003.
———. *Nisāʾ Shāʿirāt min aj-Jāhiliyya ilā Nihāyat al-Qarn al-ʿIshrīn*. Beirut: Dār al-Āfāq aj-Jadīda, 2000.
Ad-Dusūqī, Muḥammad. *Shāʿirāt ʿArabiyyāt: Ḥallaqna fī Samā ash-Shiʿr Qadīman wa Ḥadīthan*. Cairo: Dār aṭ-Ṭalāʾiʿ, 2009.

Aj-Jāḥiẓ. *Al-Maḥāsin wa-l-Aḍḍād*. Beirut: Dār aj-Jīl li-ṭ-Ṭibā'a wa-n-Nashr wa-t-Tawzī', 1997.

Al-Andalusī, Aḥmad bin Muḥammad bin 'Abd Rabbuh. *Ṭabā'i' an-Nisā' wa mā Bihā min 'Ajā'ib wa Gharā'ib wa Akhbār wa Asrār*. Edited by Muḥammad Ibrāhim Salīm, Cairo: Maktabat al-Qur'ān, 1985.

Al-'Aqqād, 'Abbās Maḥmūd. *'Arā'is wa-Shayāṭīn*. Cairo: Mu'assasat Hindāwī, 2012.

Al-Aṣfahānī, Abū-l-faraj. *Kitāb al-Aghānī*. Edited by Iḥsān 'Abbās, Ibrāhīm as-Sa'āfīn and Bakr 'Abbās, Beirut: Dār Ṣādir, 2008.

———. *Al-Imā' ash-Shawā'ir*. Edited by Jalīl al-'Aṭiyya, Beirut: Dār an-Niḍāl, 1984.

Al-Marzabānī, Abū 'Ubaidallah Muḥammad bin 'Umrān. *Ash'ār an-Nisā'*. Edited by Sāmī Makkī al-'Ānī and Hilāl Nājī, Baghdad: Dār 'Ālam al-Kutub, 1995.

Al-Wā'ilī, 'Abdul-Ḥakīm. *Mawsū'at Shā'irāt al-'Arab: Min aj-Jāhiliyya ḥatā Nihāyat al-Qarn al-'Ishrūn*, vol. 1/2, Beirut: Dār Usāma, 2001.

Aṣ-Ṣafadī, Ṣalāḥuddīn. *Al-Wāfī bi-l-Wafiyyat*. Edited by Aḥmad al-Arna'ūt and Turkī Muṣṭafā, vol. 3, Beirut: Dār Iḥyā' at-Turāth, 2000.

As-Sayūṭī, Jalāluddīn 'Abdu-r-Raḥmān ibn Abī Bakr ibn Muḥammad al-Khuḍairī. *Nuzhat aj-Julasā' fī Ash'ār an-Nisā*. Edited by 'Abdu-l-laṭīf 'Ashūr, Cairo: Maktabat al-Qur'ān, 1986.

Aṣ-Ṣūlī, Abū Bakr Muḥammad Yaḥyā. *Ash'ār Awlād al-Khulafā' wa-Akhbārahum*. Edited by J. Heyworth-Dunne, vol. 1/2, Cairo: Maṭba'at aṣ-Ṣawī, 1936.

Ibn aj-Jawzī, Jamālu-d-dīn Abū-l-Faraj 'Abdu-r-Raḥmān. *Akhbār an-Nisā'*. Edited by Nizār Riḍā, Beirut: Dār Maktabat al-Ḥayā, 1982.

Ibn Ṭaifūr, Abū-l-Faḍl Aḥmad bin Abī Ṭāhir. *Balāghāt an-Nisā' wa-Ṭarā'if Kalāmihunna wa-Milḥ Nawādirihunna wa-Akhbār Dhawāti-r-Rā'ī Minhunna wa-Ash'ārihunna fī aj-Jāhiliyya wa-Ṣadr al-Islām*. Edited by Aḥmad al-Alfī, Cairo: Maṭba'at Madrasat 'Abbās al-Awwal, 1908.

Nujaim, Jūzif. *Shā'irāt al-'Arabīya*. Beirut: Dār an-Nahār li-n-Nashr, 2003.

Shirād, Muḥāmmad and Ḥaidar Kāmil. *Mawsū'at Nisā' Shā'irāt*. Beirut: Dār wa-Maktabat al-Hilāl, 2006.

Wannūs, Ibrāhīm. *Shā'irāt al-'Arab*. Beirut: Manshūrāt Miryam, 1992.

Yamūt, Bashīr. *Shā'irāt al-'Arab fī aj-Jāhiliyya wa-l-Islām*. Damascus: Ministry of Culture, 2006.

7 Abbasid poets

1. ʿĀbida al-Juhniyya

During the Islamic holidays after Ramadan, ʿĪd al-Fiṭr, ʿAḍud ad-Dawla, King of Shīrāz and Iṣfahān, was in Baghdad, where poets were reciting celebratory poems. The poet and judge al-Kurkhī criticized ʿĀbida's poetry, so she recited a poem that combined celebratory poetry with lampoons in a brilliant blend of both genres, this time specifying the Persian new year, referred to as the Nowruz, in homage to ʿAḍud ad-Dawla,

> Al-Kurkhī asked me on the eve of the Nowruz,
> With his teeth showing in laughter,
> "What should we gift our sultan
> From the best that hands can own?"
> I told him, "All gifts are lost and useless,
> Except my advice to you:
> Give him yourself,
> So that if he lights a fire,
> You would become his Dūbārka toy."

In al-Ṣafadī, Dūbārka is explained as a popular game that children played on rooftops in Baghdad during Nowruz and other traditional celebrations.

2. ʿĀʾisha bint al-Mahdī

She is known for an encounter with Muslim ibn al-Walīd, the well-known poet whose love poetry earned him the nickname *Ṣarīʿ al-Ghawānī*, the Victim of Beautiful Women (alternatively *ghawānī* can be translated as seductresses). It is interesting how the well-established tradition of poetry challenges, *ijāza*, is reversed in this anecdote, for it was a woman this time, ʿĀʾisha, who sent a messenger to a group of poets to promise a hundred dinars to the poet who would finish the following lines she had written,

> Give us something and be generous
> For I am choking up to my throat.
> Ibn al-Walīd won the challenge by reciting,
> I am like a pail in your love,
> If I am cut loose, I would fall.

3. ʿĀʾisha bint al-Muʿtaṣim

She was the daughter of the caliph al-Muʿtaṣim, Hārūn ar-Rashīd's son. It was said that ʿĪsā ibn al-Qāsim asked her to send him one of her slaves, whom he loved. She wrote to him,

> I wrote to you and I was not modest
> For the longing of lovers cannot be held back.
> Keep her not a captive at night
> Like a man who usurps would do.

4. Al-Ḥajnāʾ bint Naṣīb

She mastered writing panegyric by visiting the caliph al-Mahdī with her father. She once visited al-Mahdī's daughter, al-ʿAbbāsa, and recited to her the following,

> We come to you, O generous ʿAbbāsa, for protection,
> As the skilled one is tired and dried out.
> The years have left us nothing,
> But a few bones heaped together.
> Someone who advised us, told us,
> Go to al-Mahdī's daughter and seek her door,
> For good settles wherever she goes.

5. Amal Jāriyat Qarīn an-Nakhās

She was a slave poet. Once, Ṣāliḥ ibn ar-Rashīd sent ash-Shatranjī to the slave merchant called Qarīn with a poem to give to a slave girl he had seen before. Ash-Shatranjī asked her, "what is your name?" She told him, "If you reach my name, you would have reached your destination." He told her,

"Then your name is Amal? (*amal* is Arabic for hope)." She laughed. He then told her, "The prince sent you this poem,"

Ask the Dominant One the Creator
Of the myriad creation and He who provides for them,
That I would not die one day separated from you.

She replied with another poem,

No, but I see you as mine and in my embrace.
If I knew your soul to be loyal in love,
I would come closer to you even if
You were on mountain top,
Whatever the messenger would say
I would tolerate.
Is there anything other
Than what they all say that I adore you?
So are we, and let the lover
With the loved one be.

The prince upon reading her poem, laughed and bought her.

6. ʿĀmil Jāriyat Zainab bint Ibrāhīm

She lived during the reign of the caliph al-Wāthiq bi-Allah. Ibrāhīm ibn al-ʿAbbās al-Ṣūlī, a poet originally from Astrabad, fell in love with her, but when he left her for a Turkish concubine, she wrote the following poem,

By God, you who breaks promises,
I wish I could trust any of this world after you.
O my shame, never would I respond
When lovers mention those they loved.

7. ʿAmmat as-Salāmī ash-Shāʿira

She was mentioned in aṣ-Ṣayūṭī's anthology as her nephew called as-Salāmī recounts that when he was a child playing in the neighborhood, she jokingly bit his cheek which hurt him, so she recited to him,

What have you done to us, you who are fond of playfulness
To a cheek that allows poetry to glow?
When I bit it with no pity, I planted a garden of violets
And turquoise crystals.

8. ʿĀrim Jāriyat Zalbahda an-Nakhās

She was from Baṣra and is known for lampoons. The poet al-Kharkī recounts to Maimūn ibn Hārūn as recorded by al-Aṣfahānī that once, while al-Kharkī was drunk, he saw ʿĀrim in the street and recited,

Would you like a phallus like mine?
And my phallus is like me.
It stands erect in front of me and stretches back behind me.
And I pound with it like a mule's phallus.

ʿĀrim chastised him with the following poem,

How about what is so narrow and hot
It would be exhausting for you inside?
If you saw it, it would stress you to death.

He said, "God knows, you shamed me," and walked away.

9. ʿĀtika al-Makhzūmiyya

She was a descendant of al-Walīd ibn al-Mughīra, Khālid ibn al-Walīd's father, and her son al-Ḥasan as-Salāmī was also a poet. She was among the poets gathering for the celebration of ʿĪd al-Fiṭr in the presence of ʿAḍud ad-Dawla. She recited the following poem in his honor,

What a difference there is between he who plans and he who destroys,
Lions hunt what the gazelles offer.
I struck fear inside him after, for a long time,
He had me mesmerized.
And I fed him what he had fed me.
I stayed up night after night,
Until I saw you, O crescent of my life.

10. Badr-l-Tamām bint al-Ḥusain

Her father was also a poet, known as al-Bāriʿ, or the Skilled One. She is mentioned in as-Sayuṭī's anthology, *Ashʿār al-nisāʾ*, for a poem she recited,

Your beauty among people is my excuse
Thinking of you during my nights is my companion.
Loving you is not complete if I am distracted,
And your love in my mind would not wander.

11. Banān Jāriyat al-Mutawakkil

She was a contemporary of the poet Faḍl. In one anecdote, she and Faḍl were accompanying the caliph al-Mutawakkil, who was leaning on both of them as they were taking a walk in the palace. He then asked them both to finish the following lines:

I learned the means of content, for angering her is what I fear,
But how to be angry is what my love for her has taught her.

Faḍl replied by reciting the following,

She rejects and I endeavor to approach by holding her dear,
She moves away and with love I would draw her closer.

While Banān recited the following,

In every way, back to her I always steer,
For I have no choice, and in that I cannot falter.

12. Bidʿa al-Kubrā Jāriyat ʿUraib

Isḥāq ibn Ayyūb at-Taghlibī was infatuated by her singing and poetry. The well-known anthologist and literary historian, Al-Aṣfahānī, recounts that she once sent Isḥāq the following greeting,

Good morrow to you my master and prince.
May you live in all blessing and bliss.
God knows my joy, bliss, glee, and pleasure,
When meeting the prince. May my life and my eyes
Are never denied meeting the prince.

Isḥāq was so pleased with her message that he sent her boxes of gifts accompanied by the following poem,

I am in a bliss with you near me,
I would give my life for yours
At times of calamity.
My joy at your proximity
Is my pleasure and my aspiration in its entirety.
May God preserve our union as long as we live
And may He keep you for me for eternity.

In another anecdote, she saw al-Muʿtaḍid coming back from war and told him that his hair had grayed. He told her that what he had seen would make anyone's hair gray. So she sang the following poem,

> If your hair has grayed, O king of the lands,
> For hard times you endured,
> Gray hair has increased your handsomeness,
> Visible gray hair perfects maturity.

He once also told her, "Don't you see how gray my hair and beard have become?" She replied by singing,

> Gray hair has harmed you none,
> But in it you grew more handsome.
> The nights have honed you,
> And you grew more complete.
> Live for us in joy,
> And, with a calm mind, your life enjoy.
> May you love life more
> Each day and every night,
> In bliss and pleasure
> And a state that grows in might.

13. Būrān bint al-Ḥasan bin Sahl

She was al-Ma'mūn's wife and her father his vizier. She wrote an elegy after her husband died,

> They caused me to weep by announcing,
> That I am now after the imam a slave to misery.
> I used to vanquish time but now time vanquishes me.

14. Danānīr Jāriyat Muḥammad bin Kunāsa

She was from Kūfa and had a poetry salon where she lived in the household of Muḥammad bin Kunāsa. A friend of his, Abū ash-Shaʿthāʾ, told her that he loved her. She recited the following poem in response,

> To Abī ash-Shaʿthāʾ a love displayed,
> That cannot be refuted nor denied.
> O my heart, shy away from him!

O the playfulness of love, sit still!
His tempting words appealed to me.
The messages of lovers are but words.
A hunter, around whom, his deer feel safe,
As if they were near the Kaʿba.
Pray and fast to God, Abā ash-Shaʿthāʾ,
If you want to be granted what you wish for.
Your date shall be on the Day of Gathering
In the Paradise of eternity, if God has mercy,
Where I shall meet you a youth in his prime,
Perfected with all blessings.

15. Faḍl ash-Shāʿira al-Yamāmiyya

Born to a free man and slave mother from al-Yamāma, it is said in some accounts that Faḍl was sold by her stepbrother after their father's death, hiding the fact that their father had acknowledged her as his daughter before his death.

Al-Mutawakkil saw Faḍl among other slave girls. He had heard of her poetry. When he first saw her, she recited the following panegyric that started his long-time protection of her,

Kingship has received the head of guidance,
In the year of thirty-three,
Following Jaʿfar,
When he was only seven after twenty,
We hope o head of guidance that you rule
For a good eighty,
May God never bless whoever
Does not say Amen,
To my prayer.

After Faḍl joined al-Mutawakkil's courtesans, he grew to trust her and value her eloquence and intelligence so much that she was present in many of his assemblies and meetings, and was even consulted in some matters.

It is said that she was once visited by al-Mutawakkil, but he was tired and fell asleep. When he woke up, she had left, and put the following poem in his sleep,

Wake up, your majesty,
Your shadow is blending in the dark.
Rise, let us melt in embraces and kisses,

Before we are seen by the return
Of slumbering souls.

In another poem, she describes him drinking in court, possibly with his wife, Qabīḥa,

Wine like a mesmerizing moon
In a cup like a bright planet.
Stirred by a young buck
Like the night's full moon
On a fresh and long shaft.

Faḍl was in love with Sa'īd ibn Ḥumaid. She wrote to him about their meeting,

You have planted your love
In my body and my soul
And it found in them
Hope mingled with despair.

When Faḍl was ill and Sa'īd did not visit her, she sent him the following message,

Patience is lacking and sickness is in sway.
And the house is near, while you are far away.
Do I complain about you,
Or to you should I complain?
For there is nothing but those two
That I can hope to gain.

16. Fāṭima bint al-Khashshāb

She is sometimes cited as an Umayyad poet and at other times as an Abbasid poet. She was once approached by her neighbor, a judge, when she moved recently there. He wrote to her,

Would the one who is longing benefit from living nearby,
While seeing visitors is not allowed?
You, who reside in my heart, and whose house
Is the goal of my sight,
You ignited my passion,
And I became young again,
After white hair had lined my beard.

She wrote back,

> If the beauty of my dress has tempted you,
> Such beauty may hide ugliness that nobody sees.
> Think not that I am matching your verse, too.
> For streams can never measure up to seas.

17. Funūn Jāriyat Yaḥyā bin Muʿādh

Ibn Zakariyya ibn Yaḥyā ibn Mu'adh recounted that his uncle had an affair with Funūn. They would exchange poems until he found out that she used to destroy the parchments where he wrote his poems after she had read them. When he reproached her for doing so, she wrote back to him explaining that she only did that to protect their secret – which apparently was too late as his nephew found out and told their story,

> You who blamed me for tearing my parchments,
> How many like you have honored me before?
> Wrapping a parchment is not enough if you were a decent person.
> Tearing it is but due to lack of trust in people.
> If you receive it and it does what it is meant to do,
> Then protect its lines from people,
> And thoroughly tear the letter of your loved one,
> For a secret may be exposed
> By the keeping of a parchment.

18. Ghuṣn Jāriyat ibn al-Aḥdab an-Nakhās

She was a slave woman freed when al-Aḥdab died. In an anecdote, the poet Daʿbal al-Khuzāʿī wanted to meet her and recited the following poem,

> Do you think time would please us with a meeting,
> And would bring together one who is longing with another?

To which she replied,

> Why speak of time, when you are time?
> So please us and let us meet.

19. Hīlāna

She was always compared to another slave girl poet, Samrāʾ, as both were in the households of rival slave traders. Once, both were asked to recite about al-Mahdī's conquests. Hīlāna recited,

My king gifted me a gown,
A dress topped by mink fur.
My pride of his gift raised my status
My joy with it spreads my light.

20. Ibnat Tamīm

A man called ʿUqba al-Asadī killed her father and was arrested for it. When she found out that her father's cousin wanted to accept money in return for dropping charges, she recited,

O people, if ʿUqaiba is killed,
He would have pleased my life and healed my illness,
O people, if ʿUqaiba is safe,
Would that serve ʿUqba.
May God curse whoever needs anything among us,
While ʿUqba is safe among us.

ʿUqaiba is a minimization of the name ʿUqba. In a sense it means Little ʿUqba. It is used here to belittle ʿUqba.

21. ʿIlm

She was mentioned in al-Arbalī's book as one of the concubines of Aḥmad ibn Yazdād. The following is one of her poems.

My fellow complained how his fine camel at night was exhausted
But didn't find he could rely on me.
He tired his ride with me in a dry spot,
Followed by effort and mounting.
A body mounted in longing every hour,
Is brought by overuse closer to its end.

22. ʿInān Jāriyat an-Nāṭāfī

Together with ʿUlayya bint al-Mahdī and Faḍl, ʿInān is among the best-known Abbasid female poets. She was bought from Yamāma by a man called Abū Khālid, who mistreated her. One poet, Marwān ibn Ḥafṣ once swore that he would free all his slaves if any of them could win a poetry contest that ʿInān was part of. No one did. It is said that she eventually was freed, either by none other than Hārūn ar-Rashīd himself in some accounts, or because her reputation as a poet had overwhelmed Abū Khālid. She even sought to either free her sisters or get herself sold to their master by writing panegyrics to Yaḥyā al-Barmakī and the Barmakids. She is particularly known for her membership in the *mājinūn* group, which was a literary salon, or *majlis*, of a more adult nature, where poets met for poetry contests, wine, and more. Since the group's name *mājiūn* means the Lewd Ones, it would be expected that their poems were all erotic. While that was partially true, their poetry was in fact just as much about wit, humor, and perhaps more significantly for the development of Arabic poetry, unprecedented experimentation with poetic devices, form, and diction that played a role in modernizing Arabic poetry, features that tend to be overshadowed by what the group's name implies.

In one anecdote, the poets decided to have a contest to choose who would host their group's subsequent meetings. After each one of them recited his poem, ʿInān recited,

> Wait, slow down, for ʿInān is a better decision and well deserved,
> At her place the best delicacies and the tastiest food is served,
> For beverages, forbidden and allowed, in my possession shall be.
> Seek no one else on earth, then, as far as eyes can see.
> Is my verdict true or not? Be honest, now, for the life of me.

The decision to grant her the honor of hosting the Lewd Ones was unanimous.

Perhaps the most interesting aspect of what survived of news about ʿInān's life was her relationship with Abū Nuwās, which seemed to have not been amorous, but a genuine friendship and comradery of two of the best poets of their age. Their poetry challenges and their poetic messages reflect a superb talent evident in the ease with which they improvised poems for countless occasions. For example, ʿInān once had company for breakfast, so she sent a handmaid to Abū Nuwās to invite him to join them with the following note,

> Visit us to eat together,
> And do not be late.
> We have decided to have our morning drinks,
> And for you we shall wait.

Abū Nuwās, not too surprisingly, slept with the handmaid, and sent the following reply to ʿInān,

> I slept with Inan's messenger,
> And that should be the answer.
> We broke bread together,
> Before the grills we ate.

Among the poetic exercises practiced by ʿInān and her circle of poets was rewriting poems, a playful exercise that also showed remarkable command of poetic form, especially as many of the poems were also put to music. One example was when al-Ḥasan ibn Wahb visited ʿInān and recited to her the following poem by another poet called Salm al-Khāsir after putting it to music,

My friend, a lover has no heart,
There is no sin in the eyes of those who see.
You who are in love, how ugly love can be,
If lover and beloved are apart.

ʿInān altered the poem using the same meter and rhyme and sang it using the same melody,

My friend, lovers have no penises,
And the loved one will have no ecstasy.
You who are in love, how ugly love can be,
If a lover's phallus has weaknesses.

It is interesting that in changing the poem, ʿInān was also lampooning chaste love poetry or *ghazal* by turning it into erotic poetry, thus playing with three major Arabic poetic genres simultaneously in a single poem, chaste love poetry, erotic poetry, and lampoons.

Just as Abū Nuwās's poetry had infinitely more depth than the playful erotic poetry that popularized him and overshadowed his genius, the same applies to ʿInān. True to the tradition of *ijāza*, Abū Nuwās once ran into ʿInān in the street and recited the following lines,

With its new daisies, each day
The earth laughs at the sky's weeping.

She finished them with the following lines,

Like a bride on a wedding day
With a dress from Ṣanʿāʾ
That the merchants are weaving.

23. Julnār bint Isḥāq

She was a singer and poet in the household of the sister of Rāshid ibn Isḥāq. She was named after the Isḥāq family. When Rāshid fell in love with Julnār, his sister locked her up and would not let him see Julnār until he paid his sister his share of an estate they had inherited. When he hesitated, Julnār thought he had abandoned her. Eventually, he could not stay away from Julnār and gave in to his sister's demands. He bought Julnār from his sister, then sent the following poem to Julnār to tell her they will be finally reunited,

The verdict has landed on the court of desertion.
Loyalty has wiped out all traces of betrayal.
In the morrow they meet under its banner,
And on it, will be hoisted the flag of victory.

Julnār wrote back to him the following,

How I feared abandonment,
Until you wrote to me your excuse.
Thus, I trust you
To make loving stronger than abandoning.

24. Khadīja bint al-Maʾmūn

She was the caliph al-Maʾmūn's daughter. She was taught poetry and music by her aunt, ʿUlayya bint al-Mahdī. The following is an erotic explicit *ghazal* poem she wrote about one of the servants in the court,

By God tell that buck with the heavy buttocks
And a waist so small,
He is sweetest when he is ready,
And, when in ecstasy,
He is the most gorgeous of all.
He built a pigeon house,
And released a dove in the loft.
I wish I were one of his pigeons,
Or a falcon,
So he could do to me what he would love.
If he wore white linen,
The fabric would hurt or scratch him
Because he is so soft.

The significance of the poem is the reversing of the stereotypical gender role in the explicit *ghazal* form as it is written by a woman about a male, thus sexualizing and even objectifying the male body. This is accentuated even further by using a buck, thus masculinizing the gazelle motif, traditionally used to describe female beauty, in order to describe the male object of the erotic poem. This is clearly the influence of Khadīja's aunt, ʿUlayya, whose poetry uses the same buck motif.

25. Khansāʾ Jāriyat al-Barmakī

She was in the household of a Barmakid man where she had a literary salon. Once, a poet called Saʿīd ibn Wahb challenged her in *ijāza* to finish the following poem,

I challenge you, Khansāʾ, with a line of poetry,
About what measures as long as a hand,
And can protect from want.
Its head has a cleft,
That leaks with what flows.
If dry, it does not run,
Neither on land nor in sea.
If wet, it brings wonders and magic.
I want no lewdness here,
I swear by the God of the last prayers of the night.
I just worded some verse
That shows some secrecy.

The Barmakid was furious and told Saʿīd, "How dare you say such lechery?" But Khansāʾ told the Barmakid to calm down and said, "He did not mean what you think. He only meant the pen," and recited her ending of Saʿīd's poem,

Abū ʿUthmān, I take the challenge of the poem you said,
For I am a girl whose poetry has cleared her head.
It appears to harbor obscenity
But there is no secrecy in what is obscene.
You meant the fast and the sensitive one,
Sharpened by whomever would seek.
In its silence it would perform
As it would run
On behalf of those who speak.
That is the pen,
Running with any matter you choose,
Be it good, or evil,
Be it harmful, or of use.

26. Khishf

She was among the entourage of al-ʿAbbās ibn al-Faḍl. She has the following short love poem,

> If you were my lot in life, I would want no more,
> I would say: He who granted me my lot has done good
> And has chosen right.

27. Khuzāmā

In al-Aṣfahānī's *al-Aghānī*, Prince Abdullah ibn al-Muʿtaz, the son of the caliph al-Muʿtaz, said that as a young man he was infatuated by the singer and poet Khuzāmā, and used to go to her to listen to songs and drink wine, and he wrote to her repeatedly but she did not write back, so he sent her the following poem,

> I see you have repented and renounced the pleasures of life.
> Wine without you has become joyless.
> I gift flowers as a reminder of life,
> With she who has not yet been separated from us by time.

She wrote back the following poem,

> I received, O Prince, verses well ornamented
> Like pearls threaded in harmony.
> Would you, son of nobility, deny me my penance,
> When time has reproached me?
> When the prime of youth has shown me,
> For the life me, that I have no excuse?

28. Lubāna bint Raiṭa bin ʿAlī

She married al-Amīn ibn ar-Rashīd, Hārūn ar-Rashīd's son, but he died before their wedding night,

> I mourn you not for the riches and high status,
> But for the glory, spear, and horse.
> I weep for a knight I grieve to lose,
> Who made me a widow before the wedding night.

29. Maḥbūba Jāriyat al-Mutawakkil

A poet and singer, she is well known mainly for her consistent loyalty to al-Mutawakkil even after his assassination, which almost cost Maḥbūba her life. Waṣīf, who took her after al-Mutawakkil's death, ordered her to sing in his assemblies but she would not sing except elegiac songs as she was in mourning for al-Mutawakkil. In anger, he threw her in prison, but she was freed later and left for Baghdad.

An example of Maḥbūba's better poems is the following description of an apple,

> O how delicious is this apple that is alone with me,
> Igniting the fire of love in my side.
> I cry to it and complain
> The sickness inflicted on me by grief.
> If an apple would cry, this one in my hand
> Would weep at my shivering.
> If you do not know what my heart has been through,
> You will find the truth inside my body.

In another poem, she mourns al-Mutawakkil, calling him by his first name Ja'far,

> What life would I enjoy, where I do not see Ja'far?
> A king my eyes saw, lying down and covered with dust.
> Everyone who has been sick has healed,
> Except for Maḥbūba, for if she saw death for sale,
> She would buy it with all she owns,
> So that she might be buried and interred.
> For the death of loved ones
> Is too good to survive.

30. Mathal Jāriyat Ibrāhīm bin al-Mudbir

A man called Ibrahim ibn al-Mudbir tells an anecdote about a slave girl he bought. When he tried to sleep with her, he could not. He recited to her apologetically,

> The one who waits may achieve what he seeks,
> And the one who rushes may err.

To this, she replied,

Maybe some people have passed what matters by waiting,
And with haste would have achieved their craving.

He said that her poem shamed him into letting her go.

31. Māwiyya al-ʿUqailiyya

She is mainly known for her love to her cousin, called Kathīr, about whom she once wrote,

Kathīr gathered himself and followed his friends
Following the shining Yamani star.
I wish, while I urge myself to be patient with promises of my wishes,
That we were all Yemeni since Kathīr is following Yaman.

Yaman is the name of star or constellation used for navigation. The poet is clearly playing on the similarity between the name of the star and the country, Yemen.

32. Mudām Jāriyat al-ʿAbbās bin al-Faḍl

She is known from a correspondence with al-ʿAbbās bin al-Faḍl, who wrote to her:

Be well, if you are busy, the heart is yours,
My endeavors with your heart are all exhausted.
If I were good at parting I would not have left you.
If I knew something other than loving you
I would not have given up.

She replied,

How many times have I used delay and hope as an excuse?
How many times have I been blamed and reproached?
How many times have I prayed that, if time set me away,
I would be guided to where my heart is and I was not guided?
Isn't it enough that sleep no longer to me finds its way,
And knocks not slowly nor rapidly?
Your letter has become wet. I studied its lines
And the trail left by tears is still on it.

33. Mukhannatha Jāriyat Zuhair

Zuhair ibn al-Musayyab, an army general, bought Mukhannatha and asked Abū Nuwās to test her. The latter asked her to finish the following lines,

> Beauty has a thing, that baffles hearts.
> There is no way to reach it,
> And there is no go-between.

She chose to finish them by lampooning Abū Nuwās himself,

> Abū Nuwās is a lecher,
> Whose words can dazzle.
> If he praises someone,
> Everyone would second.

34. Murād Jāriyat ʿAlī ibn Hishām

She was one of the few slave girl poets from Medina in Abbasid times to move to Iraq. She lived in the household of al-Maʾmūn's military general, ʿAlī ibn Hishām, joining some of the prominent *jawarī* (slave girls) of her time, such as Mutayyam, who used to compose Murād's poems into songs. When Ibn Hishām fell out of favor with al-Maʾmūn and was executed, little was known of Murād.

In an earlier anecdote, Murād was angry at Ibn Hishām and would not talk to him, so he wrote to her,

> If this really was your intention,
> Then I am healing what is between us
> With separation.
> And as a free man I shall desert you,
> For folding is better than unfolding.

In response, she wrote back,

> If you were enslaved by passion,
> Then you must be patient in spite of reluctance.
> You must close your eyelids long on what hurts the eyes,
> And obey the way a slave obeys in coercion and humiliation.
> For that is better than challenging an owner
> Who is capable of tolerating
> Separation and rejection.

35. Mutayyam al-Hishāmiyya

She was born in Baṣra and sold by Lubāna, who should not be confused with the poet Lubāna bint Raiṭa bin ʿAlī. Lubāna in this case is the daughter of al-Marākibī, the naval general assigned by Hārūn ar-Rashīd's to serve in the army led by governor ʿAlī ibn Hishām, hence her last name in reference to his household. She bore him a daughter, Ṣafiyya and two sons, Muḥammad and Hārūn. She was famous for loving flowers so much, she would tuck them in her sleeves.

Al-Ma'mūn was impressed by her, and he tested her in a poetry challenge where she wrote,

> I made my letter a lesson to be learned
> Written on the cheeks with lines of the waters of eyelids.
> My messages are many and they carry my needs.
> Here are signs of some of them with sighs.

It is said that al-Ma'mūn later arrested ʿAlī ibn Hishām and ordered that he would be put to death, possibly because he was jealous of him, but more probably because Ibn Hishām was accused of abuse of authority and corruption. Mutayyam wrote to al-Ma'mūn pleading with him to release Ibn Hishām,

> Tell al-Ma'mūn, what is your servant ʿAlī's fault,
> If he was above sins?
> He could not see beyond your integrity
> By the blessings of our Lord the King and the Protector.
> So hold your anger, and enjoy a reward
> From the Most Generous, the One who rewards.
> And use the prayer of woman under his care,
> May her prayer bring you closer to answered prayers.

Al-Maʿmūn, however, did not accept her pleading, though not only did he allow her to keep her wealth, but even freed her.

She was known even more as an admired musician than she was as a poet, to the extent that it was said that the famous musician Isḥāq al-Mawsilī attempted to falsely claim one of her compositions as among his work.

36. Nabt Jāriyat Makhfarāna al-Mukhannath

A slave girl of al-Muʿtamid. Once the poet Aḥmad ibn Abī Ṭāhir asked her to finish the following:

> Nabt, your beauty overshadows the joy of the moon.

She said,

> Your beauty almost took away my sight.
> Your scent is like musk, fanned with a garden breeze
> Late at night.

When he hesitated before finishing her lines, she beat him to the ending and said, finishing her own lines,

> May I have the good fortune of having a relationship with you,
> Or not? If I must content myself with only seeing you, I might.

37. Nasīm Jāriyat Aḥmad bin Yūsuf al-Kātib

She was the slave girl of Aḥmad al-Kātib. Once he was angry at her, and she wrote to him reproachfully,

> You showed me your wrath unfairly
> Though you are the one who forgives, understands, and forgets.
> You dominated with the power of a lord over a submissive soul.
> If it weren't because slaves submit, I would not have shown patience.
> If you contemplate what you did, you would be understanding.
> Otherwise, you will be unfair. And unfair you can be.

38. Nasīm Jāriyat al-Ma'mūn

She was one of al-Ma'mūn's slave girls. After being his favorite for a long time, he started neglecting her. When he fell ill, she sent him a gift and another slave girl with the following message,

> You break sweat leading to health,
> May God dress you in strength.
> Drink this potion, my lord, and enjoy this servant.
> And grant whoever gifted her to you a visit
> That she can enjoy the following night.

When he recovered, he took Nasīm back and she became close to him again.

39. Qabīḥa Jāriyat al-Mutawakkil

She was al-Mutawakkil's slave, then he freed her when she gave birth to his son al-Mu'taz. He was away once, and upon his return, she prepared a feast for him and sent him a message with a concubine,

You have spilled the cattle's blood seeking better health,
May God bring with it strength and health for you.
Drink, my master, this goblet
And with it enjoy this girl.
But keep some for the one who gifted her to you,
To enjoy the night that follows.

40. Qāsim Jāriyat ibn Ṭarkhān

She was a slave girl during Hārūn ar-Rashīd's time, with whom she was in love. Not much has survived of her work, but she would accompany Abū Nuwās and Marwān Abī Ḥafṣa. The poet al-ʿAbbās ibn al-Aḥnaf once asked her to finish the following lines,

His friends brought him an orange,
He cried, fearful of a bird that flew around it and would not eat it.

She replied,

He took it as a bad omen when he saw it,
For it had two colors,
Its inside differed from the outside.

41. Rayā al-Madaniyya

She was brought from al-Yamāma with another concubine, Ẓamyāʾ al-Hamadāniyya, and sold to al-Mutawakkil. When he saw them, he told them, "Recite a poem now in front of this assembly and mention me and my conquests in it." Rayā recited,

I say, and I have seen Jaʿfar's face,
The leader of guidance, and the conquest of dignity and pride,
Is this the morning sun or its likeness, Jaʿfar's face?
Is it the full moon in the sky or its likeness, the conquest?

He was pleased and decided to keep her.

42. Rayā Jāriyat ibn al-Qarāṭīsī

She was raised in Sayyid ibn Anas al-Talīdī's house. He once proudly recited,

If a youth grew up in Talīdī,
He would make the scimitar his companion in bed.

To which she responded,

A people of honor and dignity undefiled,
Time would end and their dignity would not.
God bestowed uniquely on their old and young,
Apart from everyone else, glory and nobility.
That they possess every virtue is acknowledged by everyone,
Those who deny them and those who do not.
Their ultimate pride, when they boast,
On the day of blades, is the clever Sayyid.

43. Rayā Jāriyat Isḥāq al-Mawṣilī

She was trained by Isḥāq al-Mawṣilī, a highly esteemed singer in the courts of Hārūn ar-Rashīd, a position that he inherited from his father, Ibrāhīm, and passed on to his son, Hammād, who recounted that his father was in love with Rayā. She wrote for him the following poem,

You whose embrace is delicious,
And whose departure is pernicious.
You, who is the height of my wishes,
Have taken me to approval and beyond.
I, apart from all those you see,
Am, by God, in adoration of you.

44. Rīm Jāriyat Isḥāq bin ʿAmr as-Salmī

A poet called Abū al-Yadain could not believe how good her poetry was, so he sent her two lines by a poet called Jaḥḥāf and asked her to finish them in *ijāza*,

How can I live in a land where I cannot raise my voice
If I am overcome by anger?

She wrote back to him,

How can one reside in a land
Where one fears impending doom?
Settle down in a land where people have no censor,
For a life that is censored brings one no joy.

45. Ṣafiyya al-Baghdādiyya ash-Shāʿira

She is mentioned by as-Sayūṭī and an-Nisābūrī for her poem describing her poetry. Her poem is significant in its fluidity of poetic techniques as it displays an interesting blend of pride and *ghazal* poetry,

I am the temptation of life that tempted
The depths of hearts, and they all fell in love with me so.
Would you see my face of mesmerizing beauty
And expect, whoever you are, that in peace you shall go?

46. Ṣāḥib Jāriyat ibn Ṭarkhān an-Nakhās

In his book *Female Slave Poets*, *Imā' al-Shawā'ir*, al-Aṣfahānī wrote that the poet Ibn Abī Umayya was in love with her. He wrote to her the following poem,

I saw in my dreams,
That you let me taste your cool lips,
As if your hands were in mine,
And we spent the night in the same bed.

She responded,

You dreamt well, and all that you envisioned
You shall get, in spite of those who envy us.
I hope you embrace me,
And stay on my top of breasts upright,
And we remain the most blessed lovers at night
And have a conversation with no one watching us.

47. Sāhir

She was a singer and the poet Ibrāhīm ibn al-ʿAbbās loved her. According to aṣ-Ṣafadī, their exchange of poems traces the development of their relationship. In an earlier poem, she was late for their meeting, so he recited to her when she arrived,

You for whom my longing goes
You who has my heart
You, for whom I hunger,
Whose absence leaves me with sorrow.
If you come, among all of them,
You are the one I yearn for.
Anyone else who is absent,
May be excused.

As years went by, however, he paid less attention to her. She wrote to him reproachfully,

By God, you who are a breaker of promises,
Who would be close to me and that I can trust after you?
O my shame, never have I shied away
When lovers mentioned the ones they loved.
No writer with his words tempted me.
Nor did the pleasant, the courteous, nor the eloquent.
With that tongue of yours you deceived me for a long time,
And I did not know it was just pretense.

It is said that after her poem, he never neglected her again.

48. Sakan Jāriyat Maḥmūd bin al-Ḥasan al-Warrāq

She was in the house of Maḥmūd bin al-Ḥasan al-Warrāq. She wrote a panegyric for poet Abū ʿAdnān ibn Abī Dalf,

To your heart was gifted the pain of spoilt heart,
And the reasons for sorrow.
Those eyes wherever they look,
Arrows of infatuation would fly to the heart.
Many a captive of those eyes have fallen,
Showing love, displaying passion.
His soul triumphs over the ills of souls.
He leads with graciousness, seeks no revenge.
Noble traits after they were allotted,
Yielded the reins to Dalf,
For Abū Dalf has no successor
To strength and grace,
Except Dalf.

49. Sakan Jāriyat Ṭāhir bin al-Ḥusain

Sakan was in the household of Ṭāhir bin al-Ḥusain, an important general under al-Maʾmūn during the latter's war with his brother al-Amīn. After Sakan was his favorite concubine, he stopped visiting her room. One day he told her that he was visiting her that night but never showed up, so she wrote to him,

O brave king, for you there is obedience,
For us, a grievance.
We hoped for the promised visit and waited,
But that was all we got, and a farewell.

50. Salmā al-Yamāmiyya

She joined Abū ʿAbbād's household from Mecca. He wanted to test her and challenged her in *ijāza* to finish a poem by another poet, Faḍl,

Who would help a lover who fell in love so young?
And became quite a sight as he aged?
Looking sleepless and worn,
His love is clearly shown.

She finished by reciting,

Who has someone to make them happy
During nights, long and short?
If it weren't for hope, one would have died,
And, from what I see, the soul follows one's traces.
Suffice what time has done,
Kept the hated one, to become familiar with me
Against my will.
You who left the shores of our meeting,
My longing for you is beyond my description.
You kept my eyes awake during our separation.
My eyes have enjoyed no sleep after your departure.
I sleep only to meet you in my dreams;
Though the greatest of sins
Is a woman who lost her loved one,
And yet can sleep.

51. Salmā bint al-Qurāṭīsī al-Baghdādiyya ash-Shāʿira

She was mentioned in an anthology titled *Kitāb Sīr al-Surūr* (the Book of the Secret of Pleasure) by the judge Abū al-ʿAlāʾ Muḥammad an-Nīsābūrī. He cited her poem,

The eyes of deer the color of the night yield to my eyes,
The necks of gazelles yield to my neck.
I wear necklaces though it is my neck that adorns the necklaces.
I suffer not from heavy thighs,
But of heavy breasts complain.

It was said that the caliph al-Muqtafī-li-Amr Allah read her poem and asked who wrote it. He then sent her money in appreciation.

52. Samrāʾ

She was mentioned frequently in association with another poet, Hilāna, as both usually competed in poetry contests. Once, a poet called Abū ash-Shibl al-Barjamī asked Samrāʾ to finish the following lines by Abū al-Mustahhal, who was known as the poet of the caliph Mansūr ibn al-Mahdī, writing about the battle of ʿAmūriyya (Amorium) against the Byzantine army,

> The imam built the lighthouse of guidance
> And silenced the bells of ʿAmūrīyya.

She finished by saying,

> The king dressed me in royal garb
> And topped them with the fur of mink.
> He made me proud and raised my status with his gift,
> And with its beauty lit my fire.

She later even recited two additional lines and said that would be on behalf of Hilāna,

> With this, the faith became hopeful,
> And the triggers of love were lit.

53. Ṣarf Jāriyat ibn Khuḍair Mawlā Jaʿfar ibn Sulaimān

In al-Aṣfahānī's book on female slave poets, she is mentioned as a singer from Baṣra,

> Noble he is who looks away in modesty,
> And draws near when spears are here.
> Like a sword, if you are soft, its blade softens,
> And if you are rough, then rough it would be.

54. Ṣarf Mamlūka-l-ibn ʿAmr

She is only mentioned in Majd ad-Dīn an-Nishābī's book *al-Mudhākara fi Alqāb al-Shuʿarāʾ* (Studying the Titles of Poets) in an anecdote recounting that the poet Abū al-Qāsim ʿAbd-uṣ-Ṣamad al-Muʿadhdhil wrote to her,

> I crawled fervently in the love of Ṣarf,
> For she is utterly pleasant.

Ṣarf, what say you of a lover,
Whose weeping reveals what he conceals?

And she responded,

I am at your service, Abū al-Qāsim,
You who are the goal of manners and pleasantness.
Here comes Ṣarf, who has given purely to you the gist of passion.
My love to you defies description.

55. Shamsa al-Mawṣiliyya

She was mentioned in aṣ-Ṣafadī's book as an old woman of knowledge and wisdom. The following is cited as her poem,

She sways in yellow and blue
Adorned by feathers,
Perfumed in amber and musk.
Like a spice in a garden, a flower in sunlight,
Or an image in a temple.
Graceful, when time tells her, "Get up!"
Her hips would say, wait and remain seated.

56. Ṭaif al-Baghdādiyya ash-Shāʿira

She is mentioned by as-Sayūṭī. Her poem is an example of homoerotic poems by women for women. Fewer of those poems survived than homoerotic poems by men. She wrote this poem of explicit *ghazal* for a Byzantine woman,

To a gazelle from the daughters of Byzantium
I said when we met,
"Would a lover tormented by love get a visit?"
She said, with tears flowing before words,
"If it weren't for those who would betray us,
And for the fears that concern me,
It would have been easy.
May one day it work out."

57. Taimāʾ Jāriyat Khuzaima bin Khāzim

She was a slave in Khuzaima bin Khāzim's household. According to al-Aṣfahānī, she found out he was in a relationship with a younger woman. When she reproached him, he recited the following poem,

They told me, you have loved a young one,
I told them the most delicious mount for me
Is that which has not been mounted.
Such a difference between a pearl pierced and worn
And a pearl that remained unpierced!

She replied with the following lines,

A mount is not a pleasure to mount
Until tamed by reign and mounting.
Pearls are of no use to their owners
Until threaded together and pierced.

58. Thawāb bint ʿAbdullah al-Ḥanẓaliyya al-Hamadhāniyya

Thawāb lived in Hamdān and was known for her erotic lampoons. She fell in love with a handsome merchant and married him. Yet, disappointed in him, she divorced him and wrote the following poem,

I married from Iraq a lad, who hardly had a bone,
And his little thing was also dry.
What I liked was how his hair had shone.
And the women in the neighborhood said try.
He said when we were alone
That I would groan,
But that was only because
The lad was shy.

59. Thumāma bint ʿAbdullah

As-Sayūṭī mentions her in his anthology as the daughter of ʿAbdullah ibn Siwār, a judge in Baṣra. When he died, she recited,

My eyelids dried after you,
And their ducts have flowed.
I trust time after you left.
Let disasters strike.
Your grave is watered by fresh eyes.
Woe upon you who gloat over me.
A new meadow
Appears pale in its valley.

60. ʿUlayya bint al-Mahdī

One of the most recognizable Abbasid poets, both because of the quality of her poetry, her prolific writing, and her lineage as Hārūn ar-Rashīd's half-sister. Her success links the cultural growth of the Abbasid era to the support of the court for literature and a relative empowerment for women poets. Her mother, Maknūna, was a slave in her father al-Mahdī's household, and raised her in the arts of courtesans, including poetry and music. When ʿUlayya was born, she was acknowledged as al-Mahdī's daughter. Hārūn ar-Rashīd was known to treat her as a member of the caliph's family and would ask her to join him in literary and official assemblies and reportedly would invite her to sit next to him on the throne.

Her poetry was diverse. She would alternate between chaste love poetry and sensual descriptive *ghazal*, and was among the few women poets who perfected Bacchic or wine poetry. In a poem that is often quoted for its first two lines urging the cup bearer to pour wine generously, the lines are as good as Abu Nuwās's famous lines about a similar topic. Below are the opening lines,

> Add wine to the water,
> And let me drink till I sleep.
> Pour your generosity among the people
> And become their leader.
> May God curse a miserly fellow,
> Even if he prays and fasts.

In another wine poem she wrote,

> Come then, let us have our morning drinks,
> Rejoice, and do what we may;
> Join each other for our pleasure,
> For others have let the reins go their way.

ʿUlayya was also known for her romantic escapades and her flirtations with house servants and slaves, possibly male and female, which were apparently tolerated by Hārūn ar-Rashīd. One particular member of the caliph's servants, called Ṭull, was the subject of many of her poems.

> My passion, Ṭull, for you
> Can no longer wait,
> I am visiting you now in haste,
> Treading barefoot to my doom.

It is said that Hārūn was embarrassed by her repeatedly mentioning Ṭull in her poems so he asked her to avoid mentioning the names of her lovers. In the following poem, she writes about her attempts at discretion,

I hid the name of the loved one from all people,
And repeated my yearning in my heart.
O how I long for an empty sanctuary,
Where I can call the name of my love.

ʿUlayya's love poems were not just for Ṭull. Another man, a courtier named or nicknamed Raib, was also the object of her *ghazal* poems, although some interpretations claim they were the same person,

Tell the one with the stray hair lock
On the forehead, with those cheeks
And that beautiful face,
Who set a scorched heart with the fire of love,
"It is not right what your eyes clearly did to that heart."

Her poems go beyond the traditional *ghazal*, whether explicit or chaste, that focused on the description of the lovers or on the suffering of the poet. In some of her poems she also delved into more complex psychological aspects of love, such as the following poem that tackled her inner conflict between the restraints of her royal position and her personal freedom,

I was doing my best to train myself
How, if you decide to leave, to heal.
I fought with it, till it disobeyed me
And did what you wanted,
For I have a self that is unbeatable.

In other poems, she wrote about the more classical theme of betrayal in love,

By God, if I were repaid for the good I did with good,
The one I love would not have pushed me back,
Would have not been bored,
And would have not betrayed.

And the same in the following lines as well,

I saw how people take for granted those who rush towards them.
So visit lightly and be loved more, even if you bear the pain of longing.

In another poem, she described that she was getting too old for the game of love,

I brought sleepless nights on myself,
And delved in a sea of thoughts.
Why do I need to play young and jealous?
Whoever knows love, would understand.

In a poem reflecting the Abbasid literary tradition, she writes not about lovers or a specific relationship, but about love itself, a common theme in Abbasid poetry that commented on the human condition as much as the poets' individual narratives,

So familiar with love have I become,
That love has become attached to me,
And put me on a boat to follow him.
My book cannot be read; my door cannot be seen.
Longing has set my heart on the fire of love.

Some of ʿUlayya's interesting love poems were addressed to women, Salmā and Zainab, whose identity are disputed as either female lovers or names used to refer to one of the male lovers. Classical Arab anthologists claim that those poems were meant for one of the men she loved, Ṭull or Raib, or Ṭull if both are the same man. Nevertheless, if it were outrageous for the caliph's sister to write love poetry for men, it would have probably been just as outrageous for her to write love poems for women. In that sense, it is still quite possible that those poems were indeed addressed to female lovers she had, thus making her poetry an illustration of the less common homoerotic poetry for women, such as the following,

In the heart there is a passion for Salmā
In spite of what I see of her lack of passion.
Still I wonder about wounds that persist
And do not heal,
Just like I do not see broken glass fixed.

Another poem she wrote to Salmā,

I wish Salmā would see me
Or would be told about me,
So she could free a captive
Suffering with a tired heart.

O houses of gorgeous women,
Beautiful and attractive,
The rain was generous to you
With clouds wet and sweet.

In the following poem, it is possible that the man ʿUlayya is referring to is Hārūn ar-Rashīd, trying to dissuade her from writing poetry about a female lover,

He who blames me came to me, looking away from me.
He blamed me for loving she who has a beautiful face.
I told him, by God I would not obey you with this one.
She is my soul. How can I leave my soul?
A gazelle dwelling in hills,
Grazing in pastures away from arak and wormwood.

Among the distinctive poems ʿUlayya wrote were poems about her brother Hārūn ar-Rashīd, in an interesting take on praise and love poetry within a familial context. In one anecdote, he visited her while he was stressed and overworked. It is said that she prepared musicians and dancers and sang the following song for him,

Ease my stress a little,
For I have become so thin.
Do for me beautiful things,
To make my mind spin.

Another poem addressed to her brother goes,

Your sister would give her life for you,
You have been blessed with a blessing we find
Incomparable in our time,
Except for immortality.
My being near you comes close to that, my master.
I thank God for answering my prayer.
I find my gratitude for the answered prayer still lacking.

Another poem of allegiance to her brother,

You, to whom I belong, may you be happy
And with what pleases you joyful.
I miss you, light of my eye,

Who would keep me company, my light?
May you, my master, have your word dominate
Over your enemies, and may you be victorious.

The following is another poem for her brother that also places him as her caliph as well,

You are the son of caliphs and noble ones,
By marriage and lineage.
You are offspring of the greatest,
Should the great compete
And their accomplishments compare.

In the following poem she is pleading for someone's life. It is possible that she wrote this poem as a prayer when Hārūn ar-Rashīd was sick,

By the life of my father, he is my sickness and my cure.
He is my concern, the wishes of my soul,
Whom I ask for, and for whom I plead.

During a trip she took, possibly on her way back from a pilgrimage, she stayed one night at a place called Taiz Nābādh. Her brother the caliph was upset, mainly because he suspected she was with someone, and she wrote to him to explain,

What sin have I committed, what sin?
What sin but my hope in my Lord?
By staying one day at Taiz Nābādh,
Followed by a night without drinking.
Then I followed that in the morning
With a wholesome drink
That would allure a patient monk
And make him younger.
Wine that is cold, you see, soft and mindless,
And lifts all worries.

In the following poem, she writes about how she used code to write to her lover,

We wrote in symbols amid those who were present,
Insinuations implied with no lines,
But eyes recounting their suffering
With imaginary hands on the parchments of hearts.

When she noticed people gossiping about her, she wrote the following poem,

> You who blame me, I used to blame others, too,
> Until I was inflicted and became in love and in distress.
> Love starts as a game, until it is in control,
> Then it becomes all that matters.
> I accept, and my killer is mad!
> You can wonder at this: the one who is killed is content,
> And the killer is not.

In one of her poems, she skillfully blends motifs of wine poetry with love poetry,

> A wine addict becomes sober after stupor.
> But the one in love goes through time while drunk.
> I have become drunk with no wine
> Since I remembered him, and I have never forgotten this human being.

In her poem, she masterfully reworks the traditions of campfire poetry. In this poem, it is a female speaker who remembers lost love, and an evergreen replaces the conventional desert setting,

> O garden of evergreen cypress, my yearning has lasted for too long.
> Is there a way to the shade?
> When would the one who is not allowed to go out
> Meet the one who is not permitted to go in?
> May God relieve us of this plight that befell us
> So that a friend and a companion may joyfully meet,
> And one's pain of adoration may be healed
> Of the sickness of love and its tears.

In the following poem, she claims the gazelle motif by writing a *ghazal* poem to a man and describing him as a buck, thus by masculinizing the gazelle as an objectified love interest, she also feminizes the genre of explicit love poetry,

> Give my greetings to this buck,
> Swaying in beautiful dalliance.
> Give him my greetings and say,
> "You are the lock of the hearts of men.
> You left my body exposed in the morning sun,

While you resided in the shade with doves.
You have reached a place within me
That I cannot handle."

In the following, she also claims a traditional wine poem with memories of nights of love, a type of poetry that is sometimes mistakenly associated with male poets only,

May God protect him. May we be brought together
By the Lord who is close and answers prayers.
What a good life that I and my master had,
Drinking in a cup, with fertile lands nearby.

Perhaps the following is one of the more characteristic poems of the time, normally thought of as poems that would have been written by men as it discusses a frivolous lifestyle, which shows how much agency women poets displayed in their writing,

It is all about getting younger,
Frolicking and drinking,
From wholesome wine,
In a chalice like fire.

61. Umāma bint al-Jalāḥ

A man called Miḥridh ibn Nājiya ar-Raṣṣafī was framed for corruption during the rule of the caliph al-Wāthiq and there was an order for his arrest. He escaped to the desert outskirts of al-Raṣṣāfa. There he found a house where a woman welcomed him and fed him. When he asked whose house he was in, she recited,

If you like, you can meet a man.
If you weigh him against each Muʿdī and each Yemeni
He would weigh them all in patience, grace, hospitality
And valor. That would be al-Aswad ibn Qinān.
A boy like a virgin maiden
His face shines like the sparkling of two moons.

She asked for a young man called Abū Murhaf to come and introduce himself. Miḥridh stayed in this house for a long time until al-Wāthiq's death.

62. ʿUraib al-Maʾmūniyya

She was the daughter of Jaʿfar ibn Yaḥyā al-Barmakī, and was, therefore, raised in courts, and learned poetry, singing, chess, and dice, until she became one of al-Maʾmūn's favorite courtesans to the extent that she was nicknamed al-Maʾmūniyya.

Once, Muḥammad ibn Ḥāmid was displeased with her for some reason, so she wrote to him the following poem,

You have learned my excuse, but you did not excuse me.
My body withered and you did not notice me.
You have become used to pleasure and left me.
Tears do not dry in my eyes.
After The Chosen One, no king has shown generosity
Or integrity, or protected honesty more than you have done.
May God grant Jaʿfar a long life among us,
And banish with His light the night of injustice.

The Chosen One is a translation for *al-Muṣṭafa*, which is often used to refer to Muḥammad.

When al-Mutawakkil was the caliph, he was once recovering from an illness, and she sang to him the following,

Thank He who healed you of illness
May you of pain and illness remain free.
With you the days have regained their joy,
And the gardens of generosity swayed with fruits.

In an interesting anecdote, when al-Mutawakkil's wife, Qabīḥa, was ill, he asked ʿUraib to compose a lyric and sing it to Qabīḥa but to do so in his name. ʿUraib went to Qabīḥa and sang the following,

Qabīḥa lit a fire in my heart,
And replaced my eyes with sleeplessness.
All that for her ailments.
Since she complained, I have pity for those all who complain.
She is like a white flower withering
Or a daffodil surrounded by its scent.

Qabīḥa liked the poem so much and asked ʿUraib to compose a reply to what she thought was al-Mutawakkil's song. ʿUraib used the same melody of the first song and sang the following to al-Mutawakkil as a reply from Qabīḥa,

My master you have inflicted me with sleeplessness
And taught my heart passion and fire.
If it weren't for you, I would not have felt pain for any ailment ever,
But I used my liver far too much and here it burned.
If I complained to it about my passion, it thought I was lying.
If it complained, my heart said in fear, "It is telling the truth."

The exchange of poems and songs among the caliph and his wife highlights how poetry and poets were held in high esteem in the Abbasid court, and sheds light on the virtuosity of women court poets whose talents were needed and appreciated.

63. Ẓalūm Jāriyat Muḥammad bin Muslim al-Kātib

In an anecdote by al-Aṣfahānī, the poet Aḥmad ibn Abū Ṭāhir recounts that he was visiting the poet Muḥammad bin Muslim al-Kātib and found Ẓalūm wearing a turban with the following poem sewn with golden embroidery,

I still harbor the love you have known,
Not walking away from the pledge.
That is the least I can do to obey the love I have,
And to soothe the pain of passion.

He admired the poem and asked her who wrote it. She said she did. Then she proceeded to sing it to him as well.

64. Ẓamyāʾ al-Hamadāniyya

She was brought from al-Yamāma with another concubine, Rayā al-Madaniyya, and sold to al-Mutawakkil. When he saw them, he told them, "Recite a poem now in front of this assembly and mention me and my conquests in it." Ẓamyāʾ recited,

I say when I saw Jaʿfar,
The leader of guidance, who has pride and dignity,
Is this the morning sun or Jaʿfar's face?
If the conquest is the full moon or does it just look like him?

Al-Mutawakkil then decided that he wanted only Rayā. When Ẓamyā' asked him why he would not have her, he said that she had freckles. She responded by reciting the following poem,

A buck, in all its beauty, has never been pure,
And neither was the full moon when it shone.
For the blemishes on a buck can be seen for sure,
And the spots of the moon are all well known.

After he heard her poem, he ordered her to accompany them as well.

65. Zawjat Abū Ḥamza al-Aʿrābī

A man called Abū Ḥamza was married to two women. When one of them gave birth to a girl, he was so unhappy he left for his other wife's house. The first wife wrote the following lullaby and would sing it to their daughter,

Why would not Abū Ḥamza come to us?
Why does he stay in the house next door?
Angry that we do not give birth to boys?
By God, that is not in our hands.

Bibliography

ʿAbbūd, Khāzin. *Jamīlāt al-ʿArab kamā khalladahunna ash-Shuʿarā'*. Beirut: Dār al-Ḥarf al-ʿArabī li-ṭ-Ṭibāʿa wa-n-Nashr wa-t-Tawzīʿ, 2013.

———. *Al-Musīqā wa-l-Ghinā' ʿInda al-ʿArab*. Beirut: Dār al-Ḥarf al-ʿArabī li-ṭ-Ṭibāʿa wa-n-Nashr –. *Muʿjam ash-Shuʿarā' al-ʿArab min aj-Jāhiliyya ilā Nihāyat al-Qarn al-ʿIshrīn*. Beirut: Rashād Press li-ṭ-Ṭibāʿa wa-n-Nashr wa-t-Tawzīʿ, 2008.

———. *Al-Musīqā wa-l-Ghinā' ʿInda al-ʿArab*. Beirut: Dār al-Ḥarf al-ʿArabī li-ṭ-Ṭibāʿa wa-n-Nashr wa-t-Tawzīʿ, 2004.

———. *Shuʿarā' Qatalathum Ashʿaruhum wa-Ḥubbuhum*. Beirut: Dār al-Āfāq aj-Jadīda, 2003.

———. *Nisā' Shāʿirāt min aj-Jāhiliyya ilā Nihāyat al-Qarn al-ʿIshrīn*. Beirut: Dār al-Āfāq aj-Jadīda, 2000.

Ad-Dusūqī, Muḥammad. *Shāʿirāt ʿArabiyyāt: Ḥallaqna fī Samā ash-Shiʿr Qadīman wa Ḥadīthan*. Cairo: Dār aṭ-Ṭalāʾiʿ, 2009.

Al-Andalusī, Aḥmad bin Muḥammad bin ʿAbd Rabbuh. *Ṭabāʾiʿ an-Nisā' wa mā Bihā min ʿAjāʾib wa Gharāʾib wa Akhbār wa Asrār*. Edited by Muḥammad Ibrāhim Salīm, Cairo: Maktabat al-Qurʾān, 1985.

Al-ʿAqqād, ʿAbbās Maḥmūd. *ʿArāʾis wa-Shayāṭīn*. Cairo: Muʾassasat Hindāwī, 2012.

Al-Aṣfahānī, Abū-l-faraj. *Kitāb al-Aghānī*. Edited by Iḥsān ʿAbbās, Ibrāhīm as-Saʿāfīn and Bakr ʿAbbās, Beirut: Dār Ṣādir, 2008.

———. *Al-Imā' ash-Shawā'ir*. Edited by Jalīl al-'Aṭiyya, Beirut: Dār an-Niḍāl, 1984.

Al-Heitty, Abdul-Kareem. *The Role of the Poetess at the 'Abbāsid Court (132–247/750–861): A Critical Study of the Contribution to Literature of Free Women and Slave-Girls under the Early Abbasid Caliphate: Their Biographies and Surviving Works*. Beirut: Al Rayan, 2005.

Al-Marzabānī, Abū 'Ubaidallah Muḥammad bin 'Umrān. *Ash'ār an-Nisā'*. Edited by Sāmī Makkī al-'Ānī and Hilāl Nājī, Baghdad: Dār 'Ālam al-Kutub, 1995.

Al-Wā'ilī, 'Abdul-Ḥakīm. *Mawsū'at Shā'irāt al-'Arab: Min aj-Jāhiliyya ḥatā Nihāyat al-Qarn al-'Ishrūn*, vol. 1/2, Beirut: Dār Usāma, 2001.

Aṣ-Ṣafadī, Ṣalāḥuddīn. *Al-Wāfī bi-l-Wafiyyat*. Edited by Aḥmad al-Arna'ūt and Turkī Muṣṭafā, vol. 3, Beirut: Dār Iḥyā' at-Turāth, 2000.

As-Sayūṭī, Jalāluddīn 'Abdu-r-Raḥmān ibn Abī Bakr ibn Muḥammad al-Khuḍairī. *Nuzhat aj-Julasā' fī Ash'ār an-Nisā*. Edited by 'Abdu-l-laṭīf 'Ashūr, Cairo: Maktabat al-Qur'ān, 1986.

Aṣ-Ṣūlī, Abū Bakr Muḥammad Yaḥyā. *Ash'ār Awlād al-Khulafā' wa-Akhbārahum*. Edited by J. Heyworth-Dunne, vol. 1/2, Cairo: Maṭba'at aṣ-Ṣawī, 1936.

Ibn aj-Jawzī, Jamālu-d-dīn Abū-l-Faraj 'Abdu-r-Raḥmān. *Akhbār an-Nisā'*. Edited by Nizār Riḍā, Beirut: Dār Maktabat al-Ḥayā, 1982.

Ibn Ṭaifūr, Abū-l-Faḍl Aḥmad bin Abī Ṭāhir. *Balāghāt an-Nisā' wa-Ṭarā'if Kalāmihunna wa-Milḥ Nawādirihunna wa-Akhbār Dhawāti-r-Rā'ī Minhunna wa-Ash'ārihunna fī aj-Jāhiliyya wa-Ṣadr al-Islām*. Edited by Aḥmad al-Alfī, Cairo: Maṭba'at Madrasat 'Abbās al-Awwal, 1908.

Nujaim, Jūzif. *Shā'irāt al-'Arabīya*. Beirut: Dār an-Nahār li-n-Nashr, 2003.

Shirād, Muḥāmmad and Ḥaidar Kāmil. *Mawsū'at Nisā' Shā'irāt*. Beirut: Dār wa-Maktabat al-Hilāl, 2006.

Wannūs, Ibrāhīm. *Shā'irāt al-'Arab*. Beirut: Manshūrāt Miryam, 1992.

Yamūt, Bashīr. *Shā'irāt al-'Arab fī aj-Jāhiliyya wa-l-Islām*. Damascus: Ministry of Culture, 2006.

8 Andalusian poets

1. ʿĀʾisha bint Aḥmad al-Qurṭubiyya

From Cordoba, possibly of Algerian origin. She was a calligrapher and a book collector. She was respected by al-Mudhaffar ibn al-Manṣūr and all public officials. Because she was independently wealthy, she never had to make any compromises and she never married. Her best-known poem rejecting a suitor is often quoted as an example of the agency Andalusian women enjoyed,

I am a lioness but, for the life of me,
To become someone's mount
I shall never allow myself.
And if so I ever choose to be,
A cur I would not count,
When to lions my ears were deaf.

2. Al-Bulaishiyya

Her real name is not known. She was named after Bulaish from Malaga.

I have a lover, whose cheeks
Are like roses in their whiteness.
Among people with anger he would swell,
But in private he is satisfied.
When would the one treated unfairly
Be justified,
If the unfair one is the judge as well?

Her poetry is also claimed to have been written by another poet, al-Waʾwāʾ al-Dimashqī.

3. Al-Ghassāniyya

From Bijāya (al-Mariyya). She wrote a panegyric to Prince Khairān al-ʿAmirī,

How could you be in such a state when they say
The caravans will be leaving?
Shame on you, how would you bear it, then,
When they are disappearing?
Nothing after their departure is death, then,
Unless you show patience like my patience for sorrow.
You are used to living with the shade of their love.
The gardens of love are elegant, green and blossoming.
Now that separation is happening, I wish I could tell,
Would they remain the same after separation as well?

4. Al-ʿUbādiyya

She was given as a gift to the King of Ishbīliya (Seville), al-Muʿtaḍid, the father of al-Muʿtamid. One night al-Muʿtaḍid could not sleep out of concern for some state matters, while she slept soundly, so he recited to her,

She sleeps and her lover is sleepless,
She has patience for him and he has none.

She woke up and replied,

If this lasts and it has him,
He will perish with love
Without knowing it.

5. Amat al-ʿAzīz ash-Sharīfa al-Ḥusainiyya

Ibn Daḥiyya claims her as his grandmother's sister and as a direct descendant of al-Ḥusain.

Your side looks scratch our heart,
Our side looks scratch your cheeks.
A scratch for a scratch, make this for that,
For what makes the wounds of rejection better?

6. Anas al-Qulūb

She was a slave of al-Manṣūr. One day, she recited poetry for his vizier, al-Mughīra ibn Ḥazm, in al-Manṣūr's presence,

> The night has come in the middle of the day,
> And the full moon appears like half a bracelet.
> As if the morning is a cheek,
> And darkness is a trimmed beard.
> As if the cups are iced water,
> And the wine is melting fire.
> My eyes have brought a sin upon me,
> How can I apologize for what my eyes committed?
> People, wonder at this buck,
> Wild in my love while it is next to me.
> I wish there was a way for me to him,
> To satisfy my desire.

Ibn Ḥazm responded,

> How, O how can moons be reached,
> Among dark arms and white blades?
> If I am sure your love is true,
> I would take life from you with a vengeance,
> If the noble decide to do something,
> They would risk the self and throw it in danger.

Al-Manṣūr was furious. He held his sword and spoke to Anas threateningly, "Who are you referring to with this love and longing? Tell the truth!" She said,

> If lying is more capable of saving me, truth is more deserving of telling. By God, it was only a look that brought to the heart a thought. Thus, love was spoken by my tongue, after longing left my silence. But forgiveness is guaranteed with your might, and clemency is known in your court when excuses are shown.

Then she wept profusely,

> I have committed a grave sin,
> How can I offer my apology?
> By God it was destined,
> None of it my choice.
> Forgiveness is best
> When done with power.

Al-Manṣūr then left her and turned his anger to Ibn Ḥazm who reportedly said, "May God support you! It was but a slip incited by a thought, an infatuation backed by a look. One has nothing but what is fated, rather than what one chooses and hopes for." Al-Manṣūr waited briefly then forgave them both and even gave Anas as a gift to Ibn Ḥazm.

7. Ash-Shalabiyya

Her real name is unknown and she is named after her city Shilb (Silves). She wrote to the caliph al-Muwaḥidī Abī Yūsuf Yaʿqūb al-Manṣūr around 1184 to 1199 complaining about the governor of her city and his tax collectors. In another version of the story, the poem was recited to the caliph at a Friday prayer, and he decreed to help the poet.

It is time for indignant eyes to weep
I see that even rocks are weeping.
You who are traveling to the country that we seek,
The fate of the Merciful One is taken by force.
Call upon the prince if you by his door stand,
Tell him, "O shepherd, the flock is perishing,
You send them astray and there is no pasture,
You left them prey for raiding lions.
Shilb was no city, it was a paradise,
But conquerors turned it into hell fire.
They looted and feared not God's punishment,
But nothing goes unseen by God."

8. Asmāʾ al-ʿĀmiriyya

She lived in the 12th century in Ishbīliya (Seville). She was about to lose her house to debtors, so she wrote to the caliph ʿAbdu-l-Mu'min al-Muwaḥidī asking him to pardon her of accumulating debts, and started with the following panegyric in her poem:

If we talk about the height of glory,
Your talk would take us everywhere.
You recounted his knowledge,
And honored his promise, and so it became honored.

9. Buthaina bint al-Muʿtamid bin ʿAbbād

She was poet princess, the daughter of al-Muʿtamid, king of Ishbīliya (Seville). Her mother was ar-Rumaikiyya, famous in her own right as well. Her father's palace was attacked and ransacked. She was abducted and sold to a merchant from Ishbīliya who did not know her. He gave her as a gift to his son. When the son wanted to have sex with her, she refused and told him her true name and lineage. She asked him to let her write to her father in a proper marriage proposal and wait for his reply. She sent her father the following poem with the request.

> Listen to me, and heed my words,
> For they are the thread that holds a necklace around a neck.
> Deny not that I was captured,
> I am the daughter of one of the kings of Banī ʿAbbād.
> A great king whose time has passed,
> Thus does time yield to decay.
> Hypocrisy prevailed in my father's reign,
> So separation descended and was not what I had willed.
> I went out in flight and was taken by a man,
> Whose deeds swayed from the right path.
> For he sold me like slaves are sold.
> I was taken in by someone who protected me
> From all but sorrow.
> He wanted to marry me to a noble son,
> Of good manners and traits, from Banī al-Anjād.
> He has come to you requesting your approval,
> You are the one who decides my guided path.
> May you, father, let me know,
> If he is the one suitable for my affections.
> May the Rumaikiyya of kings with her grace,
> Pray for us that we are granted blessings and happiness.

In an earlier poem, she wrote describing how her family suffered,

> There were riders who relaxed their noble rides,
> While their glory was in its prime.
> Life was quiet and let them be for some time,
> Then gave them tears of blood when it spoke.

10. Ghāyat al-Munā

Her name means the destination of wishes or the goal of all wishes. She is mentioned in an anthology by at-Tilmisānī. He recounts that Muʿtaṣim ibn Sumādiḥ asked at-Tilmisānī to recite the following lines to her and see if she could finish them,

> Ask Ghāyat al-Munā,
> "Who inflicted my body with pain."

She finished his poem with the following lines,

> "And left me infatuated?"
> Love would say, "I did."

11. Ḥafṣa bint al-Ḥāj ar-Rukūniyya

Not only is Ḥafṣa one of the most acclaimed Andalusian women poets, she is also a cultural and folkloric figure because of her tragic love story with Abū Ja'far Aḥmad 'Abdu-l-Malik ibn Sa'īd, which set them among the Arab stories of star-crossed lovers such as Lailā and Qais.

Ḥafṣa was from a wealthy family in Granada, where Abū Ja'far was a court official during the reign of al-Mu'ayyid. Their love affair was among the most public relationships at the time and shed light on a relatively more permissive community. This, however, did not last as Abū Sa'īd 'Uthmān, the governor of Granada, desired Ḥafṣa and used his political clout to target Abū Ja'far. He used Abū Ja'far's family politics to prosecute Abū Ja'far and execute him in 1163. It is possible that because Ḥafṣa was the tutor of al-Manṣūr's daughters and from a prominent family herself, that she was spared 'Uthmān's wrath. Ḥafṣa is referred to by Andalusian historian Abū al-Qāsim Khalaf ibn Bashkawāl as the Professor of Her Time.

Among Ḥafṣa's significance is how she always came through as a strong partner to Abū Ja'far. There were several notes that she left to him on various occasions where it was clear that she initiated their meetings. In example, she reshapes the image of the gazelle as the traditional passive female figure in classical love poetry, and presents herself as an eager gazelle seeking her lover,

> A visitor has come with a gazelle neck
> Yearning to the crescent under the wings of darkness.

In another poem, she uses the gazelle motif again simply calling in on her lover during work. This poem in particular sheds light on how meeting her lover was much less secretive and less complicated than poems by earlier poets that illustrate the need for secrecy in a more conservative community,

> What do you say of letting the gazelle in,
> Or maybe it is interrupting some business.

Another poem to the same effect reverses the traditional explicit love poem by having the female poet describe her own beauty and sexual promise,

> Should I call upon you, or you upon me call?
> My heart is inclined to whatever you prefer.

For my lips have nectar sweet and rare,
And the shade of all shades is my braided hair.
Answer promptly, handsome. It is not nice to stall,
For Jamīl would not have kept Buthaina waiting at all.

The reference to Jamīl and Buthaina, two folkloric lovers in classical Arabic literature, illustrates the importance of Arabic heritage in Andalusian poetry. The name Jamīl, the male lover in the classical story, is Arabic for beautiful. In the penultimate line, Ḥafṣa uses the word jamīl to refer to Abū Jaʿfar, thus linking him to Jamīl.

In another anecdote, Ḥafṣa and Abū Jaʿfar make love in a garden. He later wrote to her a poem describing the idyllic scene of their lovemaking, depicting nature as blessing the lovers' union. Ḥafṣa, however, was aware of the rising hostility against her and Abū Jaʿfar, and wrote back to him a less reassuring poem,

By your life, the meadow was not pleased by our union,
But displayed malevolence and envy.
Nor did the morning applaud, comforted by our intimacy,
Nor did the nightingale croon except for its own passions.
Make not, then, your thinking as kind as you are,
For kind thoughts are not always wise.
I do not imagine the horizon bared its stars,
For anything but to set them on us as spies.

The poem reflects not only the tragic end of Abū Jaʿfar's life, and his love story with Ḥafṣa, but also, as a late 12th-century poem, it can mirror the rising divisiveness and political corruption and turmoil towards the end of the Arab Andalusian era.

12. Ḥafṣa bint Ḥamdūn al-Ḥajāriyya

She was mainly known for her *ghazal* describing the beauty of a lover called Ibn Jamīl, which might have also been a literal nickname meaning "the son of beauty or good looks."

Ibn Jamīl saw that he sees life beautified,
For all people have been graced by
The unrestrained flow of his blessings.
He has manners like wine after it is mixed.
Better than his manners still, are his features,
With a face like the sun, calls for good omens,
And dazzles eyes with its splendor.

In another poem, she displays enough self-confidence to match her lover's,

> I have a lover who would not bend with reproach,
> And if I leave him, his arrogance would just encroach.
> He once told me, "Have you seen before the like of me?"
> So I also told him, "And do you the like of me see?"

13. Ḥamda bint Ziyād

She lived near Granada. She and her sister, Zainab, were known poets of good repute and good families. In spite of her good lineage, they would go out and join poets in their meetings out of love for poetry.

> Tears allowed my secrets to be shown to a valley
> That has traces of beauty starting to show.
> From a river that roams all meadow,
> To meadows that roams every valley.
> Among the deer, there was a fawn
> My heart felt close to her,
> My heart she stole.
> It has a side looks that she lowers for a purpose,
> And that purpose deprives my repose.
> If her hair falls and covers her,
> You see the full moon in a black horizon.
> As if a sibling has been lost to the morning,
> And in sorrow she is dressed in mourning.

14. Hind Jāriyat ash-Shāṭbī

She was the servant of the Andalusian scholar ash-Shāṭbī, who was named after Xàtiva in Valencia. She learned music and poetry in his household. She received an invitation from Abū ʿĀmir to bring her oud (a string instrument that is somewhat similar the lute) and visit him for poetry recitation and music. He wrote the following,

> Hind, would you care for a lively visit?
> We shall commit no sins, except drink nectar.

She responded by writing back to him,

> O Master, who has earned high status among
> The noble ones of the first class,

Suffice it to prove how I hasten to you,
That I am the reply returning with the messenger.

15. Huja bint ʾAbd-ur-Razāq al-Ghirnāṭiyya

She is mentioned by as-Sayūṭī as Huja and by aṣ-Ṣafadī as Muhja. She wrote the following poem,

Those who snitch would not have anything
But our separation,
Though they hold no reason for revenge
From either you or me.
They waged every raid on our ears,
And my defenders and supporters with you decreased.
I conquered them from your eyes and my tears,
And from myself with sword, flood, and fire.

16. Mahā Jāriyat ʿUraib

In al-Aṣfahānī's anthology *Female Slave Poets* (*al-Imāʾ al-Shawāʿir*), she is mentioned as the singer ʿUraib's slave. Once Sirāj al-Mālikī saw her and wrote to her,

What do I do with myself? You are my hope
A visit to you before death would revive me.

She wrote back to him,

Check your writing, for poetry can corrupt.
Poetry is the goods offered by those who have no money.

According to the anecdote, he sold a pasture for 30 thousand dirhams and freed Mahā.

17. Maryam ash-Shalabiyya

Her poetry was anthologized in *Ashʿār Ahl al-Maghrib* (The Poetry of the People of Morocco) by Ibn Dihya. She lived in Seville. It was said that al-Muhtadī was infatuated by her and wrote to her,

A pious as Virgin Mary you are,
And better than al-Khansāʾ in verse and proverbs.

She wrote back to him,

> Who can match you in words and deeds,
> You are first to show generosity without being asked.
> I can never thank you enough for the pearls
> You threaded around my necklace, and what you brought before.
> You adorned me with jewelry
> With which I boast over all women with lesser jewels.

When she was an old woman, a younger man complimented her. She replied,

> What can be hoped for from the daughter of seventy-seven years,
> Like a spider's web falling apart?
> Treads like a child, seeks her stick,
> And walks with it like a shackled lion.

18. Muhja bint at-Tiyānī al-Qurṭubiyya

Her father was fig seller. Wallāda the poet fell in love with her and trained her as a poet. Later on, however, they fell out with each other, and she wrote a bitter lampoon scandalizing Wallāda,

> Wallāda, you've become a mother with no husband,
> The secret bearer let it out.
> Mary told us something similar,
> But this one's palm tree is an actual man.

In one of her poems, she describes how she is capable of protecting herself, and choosing who to kiss or even have sex with. Her poem shows the influence of Wallāda's famous poem about choice,

> If she pushes away those who swarm around her lips,
> Other openings are also protected from those who aspire them,
> The former is protected by cutters and blades,
> The latter are protected by the magic of looks.

Once, an admirer gave her peaches as a gift. She wrote a lampoon and sent it to him,

> You who gifted peaches to his beloved,
> It is welcome to cool my chest.

Rounded like a beauty's breast,
But it shames a phallus's head.

19. Mutʿa al-Andalusiyya

She was a slave at the singer Ziryāb, who taught her music so she would set melodies for her poems and sing them. Once she accompanied Ziryāb on a visit to Prince ʿAbd-ur-Raḥmān ibn al-Ḥakam. She noticed how the Prince liked her but would not show it, so she recited,

You who conceals his love,
Who can conceal the morning?
I used to own my heart,
Until I was in love entangled,
Then it flew away.
Woe upon me, was it really mine,
Or was fake?
By the life of my father,
For him, my modesty I forsake.

It was said that, upon hearing that, Ziryāb gifted her to the Prince. The anecdote is an example of how slave women used poetry to achieve a certain degree of social mobility as she, while still a slave, managed to move from the house of a singer to that of a prince.

20. Nuzhawn bint al-Qilāʿī al-Ghirnāṭiyya

She was one of the most accomplished Andalusian female poets, and it is possible to see her as one of the three best Andalusian women poets together with Ḥafṣa ar-Rakūniyya and Wallāda Bint al-Mustakfī. She had a literary salon where she recited poetry and gave lectures. She was promiscuous and did not hide that fact. The vizier Abū Bakr ibn Saʿīd was infatuated by her and attended all her literary salon meetings. He once wrote to her,

You who have a thousand intimate ones,
From lovers to friends,
I see you have prepared a house
For people in the road.

She replied,

> Abū Bakr you landed in a place
> Just for you and I denied the rest.
> Who but my lover would
> Have my breast?
> If I have more than one lover,
> Those who are fair know
> Abū Bakr's love comes first.

She once challenged another poet and asked him to finish the following line,

> If you saw who you were talking to

He could not, so she finished it herself,

> You would go mute to his bangles.
> The full moon rises in his tunic,
> The branch plays in his under garments.

21. Qamar al-Ishbīliyya

Originally from Baghdad, she was gifted to Ibrāhīm ibn Hajjāj, the governor of Seville. Her name means the Moon of Seville. In an anecdote about the Andalusian court, it was said that other slave women ridiculed her for coming from Baghdad and accused her of being a social climber and an opportunist, which highlights class and ethnic tensions among Mediterranean and Andalusian Arabs on the one hand and Asian Arabs on the other hand. Qamar responded to those making fun of her by reciting,

> They said: "Qamar came in rags,
> After her eyelashes slashed a heart.
> She treads in dread, she walks early,
> Crossing lands and countries over countries.
> She is not free to choose her setting.
> She has nothing but rhymes and poems."
> If they were sensible, they would not have shamed the stranger.
> May God help a slave girl hurt by those who are free.
> The child of Adam has nothing but hard work,
> After faith and loyalty to the Creator.
> Let me be, away with ignorance, I shall not tolerate its bearers.

Ignorance will never run out of shaming and insults.
If there was no Paradise but for those who are ignorant,
I would be content from the Lord of the people with hell.

22. Qasmūna bint Ismāʿīl

She was a Jewish Andalusian poet and is often cited as an example of the religious harmony in the Andalusian Arab community. Her father Ismāʿīl ibn Naghrīla was a poet as well. Once he asked her to finish the following lines,

I have a companion of pleasure,
Who met my blessings with injustice,
Justifying her crime.

She did by reciting the following,

Like the sun, whose light the moon always steals,
Then eclipses its body.

In another incident, it was said she was admiring herself in the mirror and recited a poem critiquing conservative traditions that would not allow sex before marriage,

I see a garden ripe for picking,
But see no picker reaching out to pick.
Alas! Youth goes wasted,
And what I shall not name remains single.

In one of her best poems, she compares herself to a deer, thus engaging with the classical metaphor of gazelles in Arabic poetry, while also gaining agency by describing herself as a gazelle rather than allowing herself to become objectified if she is described by a male poet as a gazelle,

O deer that always grazes at the pasture,
I resemble you in loneliness and in eyes so dark.
The evening has come to both of us single without a companion,
Let us, then, be patient forever with what fate decrees.

23. Ṣafiyya bint ʿAbdallah ar-Raibī

She was known for her calligraphy. Al-Ḥumaidī said in *al-Muqtabas fi Dhikr Wulāt al-Andalus* that a woman once criticized Ṣafiyya's calligraphy, so she replied,

For she who criticized my handwriting, I said,
"Come closer, I shall show you in verse my lines."
I signaled to her so she can grace me with her handwriting,
And drew near my pens, paper, and ink.
She wrote down three lines of my verse,
Then I told her, "Here, look."

24. Ṣafiyya bint ʿAbd-ur-Raḥmān

She was known for her wisdom and bringing the scenic al-Andalus in her poems. She once asked the poet Ibn an-Najjār to finish the following two lines,

If a land is empty of my loved ones,
Its valley does not flow and its branches do not turn green.

When he could not, she finished them herself,

No neighbor in the quarter after you has uttered
What pleases me with song or hymn.
I weep the quarter since its people have left,
And seek nights that ended. Who would bring them back?

25. Tamīma bint Yūsuf bin Tāshfīn

She was also known as Umm Ṭalḥa. Her poetry is also claimed to have been written by al-ʿAbbās ibn al-Aḥnaf,

It is the sun, its home is in the skies,
So console your heart and soothe it,
For neither can you to it ascend,
Nor can it descend to you.

26. Umm al-ʿAlāʾ al-Ḥujāriyya al-Barbariyya

She lived in the Valley of Rocks, Wādī al-Ḥijāra, hence her name. She was originally from the Berber of North Africa. She wrote the following poem,

Anything that comes from you is good,
With your grace, time is adorned.
The eye looks kindly at your appearance,

The ears are pleased by your memory.
Whoever lives without you in their lives
Is unfairly treated and of wishes deprived.

In another poem, she wrote,

O morning do not appear to my darkness,
For the night cannot with the morning stay.
Youth cannot do anything for graying hair,
My advice do heel.
Do not be the most ignorant of people,
Living in ignorance night and day.

27. Umm al-Hanāʾ

She was the daughter of the judge Abū Muḥammad ʿAbdu-l-Ḥaq bin ʿAṭiyya. When he was appointed judge of al-Mariyya, he came home in tears at having to leave her in their home city. Later, when she received a letter from him announcing that he would visit her soon, she wrote back,

The letter arrived from my dear one,
That he is visiting me, so my eyes teared up.
Joy overwhelmed me so much,
That, out of pleasure, it made me weep.

Knowing how short his visit would be, she recited,

Receive as good omen the day you shall meet him,
And leave the tears for the night of departure.

When she received him, she recited,

O eyes that have made tears a habit,
Weeping in joy as in sadness.

28. Umm al-Ḥasan bint Abī Jaʿfar aṭ-Ṭanjālī

She was the daughter of the judge Abū Jaʿfar aṭ-Ṭanjālī from Lucia. Her family later moved to Malaga. Her father took considerable care in educating her in various disciplines, especially medicine. Once, he returned from travels in Morocco and wanted to test his daughter's progress during his absence. He asked her about her skill in calligraphy, which apparently was not strong. She replied with the following lines:

Calligraphy is of no use to knowledge,
But an adornment on parchment.
Studying is what I seek, and would not replace,
As much as one knows, as high as they would rise.

29. Umm al-Kirām bint al-Muʿtaṣim bin Ṣamāḍiḥ

She is the daughter of al-Muʿtaṣim bi-Allah, king of al-Mariyya. She was in love with a young man famous for his handsomeness, known as as-Sammār. She wrote about him the following lines,

People, you may wonder at what the scourge of love has done.
If it were not for love, the full moon would not descend
From its high seat to the dust.
Suffice it for me that, if my loved one left me,
My heart will follow.

30. Umm as-Saʿd bint ʿIṣām al-Ḥumairī (Saʿdūna)

She was also known as Saʿdūna. She was from a Cordovan family of poets and scholars. Her sister, Muhja, is a poet in her own right as well. It is said that either her father or grandfather once recited in praise of the Prophet,

I shall kiss the statue,
If I cannot find a way to kiss the Prophet's shoes.

She finished the poem with the following lines,

May I be granted the honor of kissing it,
In Paradise, is better said.
In the good shade, resting and safe,
Drinking from cups of the sublime drink (Salsabīl),
Touch my heart with it,
May it calm down its angst.
For healing with the remains of loved ones,
Has long been sought by lovers
From all generations.

31. Wallāda bint al-Mustakfī bi-Allah

One of the most respected Andalusian women poets, she was famous as much for the quality of her poetry as for the agency and empowerment she consciously displayed. She became an iconic cultural figure of Andalusian community when she embroidered in golden threads a couplet on her dress, one line on each side. The poem itself expresses an unmistakable statement on female sexual choices,

> I, by God, am good for a high state,
> I walk my walk and swagger with a proud gait.
>
> I enable my lover to have my whole cheek,
> And give a kiss to whomever my kiss would seek.

In addition to her poetry, Wallāda was known for her relationship with Ibn Zaidūn, lampooning him for his infidelities at times, and writing him love poems at others. Asking him to prepare for her visit, she once sent him the following poem, which has been frequently quoted in various occasions to denote a couple's secret meeting or rendezvous,

> Await my visit, when darkness prevails.
> I see the night a better keeper of secrets.
> And I have with you what would
> Make the sun not rise,
> The moon not shine,
> And the stars not travel.

In another occasion, she learned of his affair with another woman, and possibly another man, so she wrote to him,

> It is I who am the full moon of the sky, you know.
> Yet, woe unto me,
> It is Jupiter that you are fond of, though.

32. Zainab bint Farwa al-Mariyya

She is mentioned by ibn al-Jawzī in *Akhbār al-Nisā'*.

> You who are riding your mount early,
> Come here that I might tell you what I find:
> People have not had passions that enwrapped them,

That were not exceeded by my passion.
Suffice it for me that he would be content,
And, for his pleasure and good company,
I would labor for the last of days.

33. Zainab bint Isḥāq an-Naṣrānī

Her lineage goes back to Ra'ˀs al-ʿAin in Al-Andalus. Her poetry survived through the linguist Rāḍī ad-Dīn known as ash-Shaṭibī.

As for ʿAdī and Tayyim, I try not to mention them with misgivings,
But I love Hāshim.
What overwhelms me when it comes to ʿAlī and his kin,
If they are mentioned with blame,
People say, "Why do Christians love them,
And thinkers among Arabs and foreigners?"
I would say to them, "I believe their love
Has traveled in the hearts of all creatures,
Including beasts."

Bibliography

ʿAbbūd, Khāzin. *Jamīlāt al-ʿArab kamā khalladahunna ash-Shuʿarāʾ*. Beirut: Dār al-Ḥarf al-ʿArabī li-ṭ-Ṭibāʿa wa-n-Nashr wa-t-Tawzīʿ, 2013.

———. *Muʿjam ash-Shuʿarāʾ al-ʿArab min aj-Jāhiliyya ilā Nihāyat al-Qarn al-ʿIshrīn*. Beirut: Rashād Press li-ṭ-Ṭibāʿa wa-n-Nashr wa-t-Tawzīʿ, 2008.

———. *Al-Musīqā wa-l-Ghināʾ ʿInda al-ʿArab*. Beirut: Dār al-Ḥarf al-ʿArabī li-ṭ-Ṭibāʿa wa-n-Nashr wa-t-Tawzīʿ, 2004.

———. *Shuʿarāʾ Qatalathum Ashʿaruhum wa-Ḥubbuhum*. Beirut: Dār al-Āfāq aj-Jadīda, 2003.

———. *Nisāʾ Shāʿirāt min aj-Jāhiliyya ilā Nihāyat al-Qarn al-ʿIshrīn*. Beirut: Dār al-Āfāq aj-Jadīda, 2000.

Ad-Dusūqī, Muḥammad. *Shāʿirāt ʿArabiyyāt: Ḥallaqna fī Samā ash-Shiʿr Qadīman wa Ḥadīthan*. Cairo: Dār aṭ-Ṭalāʾiʿ, 2009.

Al-Andalusī, Aḥmad bin Muḥammad bin ʿAbd Rabbuh. *Ṭabāʾiʿ an-Nisāʾ wa mā Bihā min ʿAjāʾib wa Gharāʾib wa Akhbār wa Asrār*. Edited by Muḥammad Ibrāhim Salīm, Cairo: Maktabat al-Qurʾān, 1985.

Al-ʿAqqād, ʿAbbās Maḥmūd. *ʿArāʾis wa-Shayāṭīn*. Cairo: Muʾassasat Hindāwī, 2012.

Al-ʿAzzāwī, Turkī. *Muʿjam Shāʿirāt al-Andalus maʿa Raqāʾiq Mustaʿdhaba min Shiʿrihunna ar-Rāʾiʿ*. Damascus, Beirut and Kuwait: Dār an-Nawādir, 2012.

Al-Maghribī, Abū al-Ḥasan ʿAlī ibn Saʿīd. *Al-Maghrib fī ḥulī al-Maghrib*. Edited by Shawqī Ḍaif, Cairo: Dār al-Maʿārif, 1955.

Al-Wāʾilī, ʿAbdul-Ḥakīm. *Mawsūʿat Shāʿirāt al-ʿArab: Min aj-Jāhiliyya ḥatā Nihāyat al-Qarn al-ʿIshrūn*, vol. 1/2, Beirut: Dār Usāma, 2001.

Aṣ-Ṣafadī, Ṣalāḥuddīn. *Al-Wāfī bi-l-Wafiyyat*. Edited by Aḥmad al-Arnaʾūt and Turkī Muṣṭafā, vol. 3, Beirut: Dār Iḥyāʾ at-Turāth, 2000.
As-Sayūṭī, Jalāluddīn ʿAbdu-r-Raḥmān ibn Abī Bakr ibn Muḥammad al-Khuḍairī. *Nuzhat aj-Julasāʾ fī Ashʿār an-Nisā*. Edited by ʿAbdu-l-laṭīf ʿAshūr, Cairo: Maktabat al-Qurʾān, 1986.
At-Tilmisānī, Aḥmad bin Muḥammad al-Maqrī. *Nafḥu aṭ-Ṭīb min Ghuṣn al-Andalus ar-Raṭīb*. Edited by Iḥsān ʿAbbās, vol. 1/2, Beirut: Dār Ṣādir, 1968.
Ibn aj-Jawzī, Jamālu-d-dīn Abū-l-Faraj ʿAbdu-r-Raḥmān. *Akhbār an-Nisāʾ*. Edited by Nizār Riḍā, Beirut: Dār Maktabat al-Ḥayā, 1982.
Nujaim, Jūzif. *Shāʿirāt al-ʿArabīya*. Beirut: Dār an-Nahār li-n-Nashr, 2003.
Shirād, Muḥāmmad and Ḥaidar Kāmil. *Mawsūʿat Nisāʾ Shāʿirāt*. Beirut: Dār wa-Maktabat al-Hilāl, 2006.
Wannūs, Ibrāhīm. *Shāʿirāt al-ʿArab*. Beirut: Manshūrāt Miryam, 1992.
Yamūt, Bashīr. *Shāʿirāt al-ʿArab fī aj-Jāhiliyya wa-l-Islām*. Damascus: Ministry of Culture, 2006.

9 Fatimid and Mamluk poets

1. ʿĀʾisha al-Bāʿūniyya

ʿĀʾisha bint Yūsuf ibn Aḥmad al-Bāʿunī's lineage goes back to Bāʿūn, a family from ʿAjlūn in Jordan. She was born in Damascus, but lived in Egypt, then returned to Aleppo later in her life before her death in Damascus.

She wrote Sufi poetry in praise of Prophet Muḥammad,

A prophet cleansed by God with His sublime light.
No throne nor miracle need be named.
He forged creation for his sake,
So His mercy may be claimed.
He granted only him what He would grant from only Him.
Planted a secret in him.
With knowledge He would fill him.
Showed him the Self,
To him,
All beauty he would teach.
He fitted him with wisdom,
And His side,
He enabled him to reach.

2. ʿĀʾisha bint ʿImāra al-Ḥusnī

A Moroccan poet and calligrapher. It is said she copied the entire 18 or 20 volumes of al-Thaʿālibī's *Kitāb Yatīmat ud-Dahr*.

She was known for wit and wordplay. She once wrote to poet Abū al-Ḥasan al-Fakkūn a short poem and challenged him to finish them. He declared he could not and said, "To stop at those two lines would be the right thing to do." This is the poem she wrote that he could not finish:

They took my heart and left me.
Of me

My longing is now a part.
If they do not return, forgive me.
Or from me
You must stay apart.

3. Al-Badawiyya (The Bedouin)

Sometimes referred to in literary works as Salmā but is mainly known as the Bedouin, she is best known in Egyptian folklore for her role in the love triangle that involved the Fatimid caliph Manṣūr al-Āmir bi-Aḥkām-il-lāh and her cousin, Ibn Mayyāḥ. She was from the south of Egypt where she was in love with her cousin when the caliph saw her during his visit to the southern parts of Egypt. He became so infatuated with her that he married her and built for her a palace in Fusṭāṭ shaped like a howdah, which in folklore is given the name the Howdah Palace, but it is not historically confirmed.

Al-Āmir was assassinated in that palace in 1130. In some accounts, her cousin, Ibn Mayyāḥ, eventually disappeared. She recited the following poem to Ibn Mayyāḥ from the palace,

Ibn Mayyāḥ, to you my complaint would be.
An owner after you now owns me.
In my body you roamed sovereign and free,
Having what you desired wantonly.
But now in a locked palace I reside,
Where I only see a vile one
With no stride.

4. Badīʿa ar-Rifāʿiyya

Badīʿa bint Sirāj-ud-Dīn ar-Rifāʿī was a Sufi poet, possibly from the Rifāʿī family that is linked to the ar-Rifāʿī Sufi order in Cairo. She wrote in praise of Muḥammad,

O messenger of guidance, I call you with a heart
Submissive and fearful,
O upon the garden of Aḥmad,
Are my greetings, although
So humble is my effort
That of worthy greetings it falls short.
For you are the lantern of all existence,
And the sun on the face of guidance to the earth.

5. Fāṭima bint al-Khashshāb

She possibly lived in between Damascus and Cairo. She was a contemporary of Ṣalāḥ-ud-Dīn aṣ-Ṣafadī (b.1296) and lived under the Mamluk sultan an-Nāṣir Muḥammad ibn Qalāwūn (1285–1341). It is said that the judge Shihāb-ud-Dīn ibn Faḍl either lived near her house or that he visited her late but was denied entry so he wrote to her once,

What use is proximity to a beloved's home,
If "Not Allowed" is all that visitors are ever told?
You who are the guest of my heart,
Whose house my eyes long to behold,
Have aroused my passion and brought youth back to me,
After white hair in my beard has been roaming free.

Fāṭima wrote back to him,

If the beauty of my dress your heart holds,
Beware that ugliness is hidden in its folds.
Think not that my verse like yours can be,
For who can compare a humble stream
To the sea?

6. Fāṭima bint Muḥammad ibn Shīrīn Al-Ḥanafī

Fāṭima's second husband was al-ʿAlāʾ ibn Muḥammad ibn Baibars, a descendant of aẓ-Ẓāhir Baibars, the fourth Mamluk sultan of Egypt. She lived and died in Cairo and was known for corresponding with intellectuals of her time.

She wrote a poem in praise of piety,

Stop and listen to my words, my dear ones,
The features of their beauty are displayed:
Those who obeyed God, and their hearts were lit,
Saw things they were not told,
To them all intent would unfold.
Their hearts are lit
With the insights that they hold.

7. Taqiyya bint Ghaith aṣ-Ṣūriyya

Born in Damascus, she lived and died in Alexandria. She studied with an imam and reciter known as ʿAbd-uṭ-Ṭahir Aḥmad bin Silfī al-Aṣbahānī, known as as-Silfī (478–1180). He recounted that he once stubbed his toe and a young woman from the household ripped part of her scarf to bandage his toe. Taqiyya was there and wrote,

If I were to find a way,
For the scarf of this girl
I would have given my cheek instead.
Were I would kiss today the foot
That on the praised path does tread.

Another reciter, Zakī-ud-Dīn al-Mundhirī recounts that Taqiyya once wrote a Bacchic poem as a panegyric for Ṣalāḥ-ud-Dīn's cousin, Muẓaffar ʿUmar. Muẓaffar said that she must have experienced wine to be able to describe it so accurately. In response, she wrote a war poem with details of battle and sent the poem to Muẓaffar with the message, "My knowledge of this is the same as my knowledge of the other."

She also wrote,

I refused but my heart with refusal is not content,
So do not take my denial as my true intent.
For them I long and with them I am enamored,
Though they stabbed my heart with spears so broad.
When I remember the Levant and its people,
With tears of blood I weep, for the time that went.

Bibliography

ʿAbbūd, Khāzin. *Jamīlāt al-ʿArab kamā khalladahunna ash-Shuʿarāʾ*. Beirut: Dār al-Ḥarf al-ʿArabī li-ṭ-Ṭibāʿa wa-n-Nashr wa-t-Tawzīʿ, 2013.

———. *Al-Musīqā wa-l-Ghināʾ ʿInda al-ʿArab*. Beirut: Dār al-Ḥarf al-ʿArabī li-ṭ-Ṭibāʿa wa-n-Nashr –. *Muʿjam ash-Shuʿarāʾ al-ʿArab min aj-Jāhiliyya ilā Nihāyat al-Qarn al-ʿIshrīn*. Beirut: Rashād Press li-ṭ-Ṭibāʿa wa-n-Nashr wa-t-Tawzīʿ, 2008.

———. *Al-Musīqā wa-l-Ghināʾ ʿInda al-ʿArab*. Beirut: Dār al-Ḥarf al-ʿArabī li-ṭ-Ṭibāʿa wa-n-Nashr wa-t-Tawzīʿ, 2004.

———. *Shuʿarāʾ Qatalathum Ashʿaruhum wa-Ḥubbuhum*. Beirut: Dār al-Āfāq aj-Jadīda, 2003.

———. *Nisāʾ Shāʿirāt min aj-Jāhiliyya ilā Nihāyat al-Qarn al-ʿIshrīn*. Beirut: Dār al-Āfāq aj-Jadīda, 2000.

Ad-Dusūqī, Muḥammad. *Shāʿirāt ʿArabiyyāt: Ḥallaqna fī Samā ash-Shiʿr Qadīman wa Ḥadīthan*. Cairo: Dār aṭ-Ṭalāʾiʿ, 2009.

Al-ʿAqqād, ʿAbbās Maḥmūd. *ʿArāʾis wa-Shayāṭīn*. Cairo: Muʾassasat Hindāwī, 2012.

Al-ʿAzzāwī, Turkī. *Muʿjam Shāʿirāt al-Andalus maʿa Raqāʾiq Mustaʿdhaba min Shiʿrihunna ar-Rāʾiʿ*. Damascus, Beirut and Kuwait: Dār an-Nawādir, 2012.

Al-Maghribī, Abū al-Ḥasan ʿAlī ibn Saʿīd. *Al-Maghrib fī ḥulī al-Maghrib*. Edited by Shawqī Ḍaif, Cairo: Dār al-Maʿārif, 1955.

Al-Wā'ilī, 'Abdul-Ḥakīm. *Mawsū'at Shā'irāt al-'Arab: Min aj-Jāhiliyya ḥatā Nihāyat al-Qarn al-'Ishrūn*, vol. 1/2, Beirut: Dār Usāma, 2001.

Aṣ-Ṣafadī, Ṣalāḥuddīn. *Al-Wāfī bi-l-Wafiyyat.* Edited by Aḥmad al-Arna'ūt and Turkī Muṣṭafā, vol. 3, Beirut: Dār Iḥyā' at-Turāth, 2000.

As-Sayūṭī, Jalāluddīn 'Abdu-r-Raḥmān ibn Abī Bakr ibn Muḥammad al-Khuḍairī. *Nuzhat aj-Julasā' fī Ash'ār an-Nisā.* Edited by 'Abdu-l-laṭīf 'Ashūr, Cairo: Maktabat al-Qur'ān, 1986.

At-Tilmisānī, Aḥmad bin Muḥammad al-Maqrī. *Nafḥu aṭ-Ṭīb min Ghuṣn al-Andalus ar-Raṭīb.* Edited by Iḥsān 'Abbās, vol. 1/2, Beirut: Dār Ṣādir, 1968.

Ibn aj-Jawzī, Jamālu-d-dīn Abū-l-Faraj 'Abdu-r-Raḥmān. *Akhbār an-Nisā'.* Edited by Nizār Riḍā, Beirut: Dār Maktabat al-Ḥayā, 1982.

Nujaim, Jūzif. *Shā'irāt al-'Arabīya.* Beirut: Dār an-Nahār li-n-Nashr, 2003.

Shirād, Muḥāmmad and Ḥaidar Kāmil. *Mawsū'at Nisā' Shā'irāt.* Beirut: Dār wa-Maktabat al-Hilāl, 2006.

Wannūs, Ibrāhīm. *Shā'irāt al-'Arab.* Beirut: Manshūrāt Miryam, 1992.

Yamūt, Bashīr. *Shā'irāt al-'Arab fī aj-Jāhiliyya wa-l-Islām.* Damascus: Ministry of Culture, 2006.

Index